200

"There's no question a gigantic trauma is coming, and many debts are going to be wiped out... This is going to end badly."
– Interview with legendary investor Jim Rogers

THE AMERICAN JUBILEE

A NATIONAL NIGHTMARE IS CLOSER THAN YOU THINK

PORTER STANSBERRY

STANSBERRY
RESEARCH

Published by Stansberry Research

Edited by Fawn Gwynallen

Designed by Lauren Thorsen

About Stansberry Research

Founded in 1999 and based out of Baltimore, Maryland, Stansberry Research is the largest independent source of financial insight in the world. It delivers unbiased investment advice to self-directed investors seeking an edge in a wide variety of sectors and market conditions.

Stansberry Research has nearly two dozen analysts and researchers – including former hedge-fund managers and buy-side financial experts. They produce a steady stream of timely research on value investing, income generation, resources, biotech, financials, short-selling, macroeconomic analysis, options trading, and more.

The company's unrelenting and uncompromised insight has made it one of the most respected and sought-after research organizations in the financial sector. It has nearly 200 employees operating in several offices in the U.S. plus one in Asia, and it serves 350,000 customers in more than 120 countries.

About the Author

 Porter Stansberry founded Stansberry Research in 1999 with the firm's flagship newsletter, *Stansberry's Investment Advisory*. He is also the co-host of *Stansberry Investor Hour*, a broadcast that has quickly become one of the most popular online financial radio shows.

Prior to launching Stansberry Research, Porter was the first American editor of the *Fleet Street Letter*, the world's oldest English-language financial newsletter.

Today, Porter is well-known for doing some of the most important – and often controversial – work in the financial advisory business. His string of accurate forecasts has made *Stansberry's Investment Advisory* one of the most widely read financial newsletters in the world, and has helped his readers both avoid catastrophe and make incredible gains.

For example, his dead-on prediction of the mortgage meltdown got the attention of Barron's, who said Porter's work was "remarkably prescient... Nothing, as far as we can see, has happened to contradict his dire prophecy..."

At Stansberry Research, Porter oversees more than a dozen of the best editors and analysts in the business, who do an exhaustive amount of real-world, independent research. Together, his group has visited hundreds of publicly traded companies to bring Stansberry Research subscribers the safest, most profitable investment ideas in the world, no matter what's happening in the markets.

Table of Contents

Part IV
How to Own the World's Trophy Assets

Part V
Porter Stansberry's Crash Course on How to Become a Better Investor

Part VI
How to Earn Crisis-Proof, Inflation-Proof Income Streams in the Stock Market

– Introduction –

Porter Stansberry
Founder, Stansberry Research

A major Jubilee is coming to America... soon.

Lots of people will be excited about this once-in-50-years event. The crowds will cheer. And politicians will promise new and better prosperity.

But what will actually happen is a national nightmare.

If you've never heard of the concept of a national Jubilee, I urge you to read this book carefully and skeptically.

You see, I fear we may be among the only people in America who know what's about to happen... and why it can't be stopped.

Did you ever read Shirley Jackson's acclaimed short story, *The Lottery?*

The story starts out by painting a picture of a beautiful, small farming community.

> The morning of June 27th was clear and sunny, with the fresh warmth of a full-summer day; the flowers were blossoming profusely and the grass was richly green. The people of the village began to gather in the square, between the post office and the bank, around ten o'clock... The children assembled first, of course. School was recently over for the summer, and the feeling of liberty sat uneasily on most of them; they tended to gather together quietly for a while before they broke into boisterous play.

The author, however, soon hints at the depravity that will follow...

> Bobby Martin had already stuffed his pockets full of stones, and the other boys soon followed his example, selecting the smoothest and roundest stones; Bobby and Harry Jones and Dickie Delacroix – the villagers pronounced this name "Dellacroy" – eventually made a great pile of stones in one corner of the square and guarded it against the raids of the other boys.

This is a lottery that no one wants to win.

As you know if you've ever read the story, every adult has to draw a card from the black box. Whoever pulls out the card with the mark of death (a black spot) is stoned to death. It's a ritual killing. Every member of the community must take part. They even hand a stone to the victim's young son, so he can take part in the ritual.

The Jubilee we're about to experience will have many of the same characteristics...

Millions of Americans will soon be calling for it. Some violently. The young, the poor, and the ignorant will all rally for Jubilee. They will, in effect, start piling up stones. And the person who is going to be ritually killed? That will be us.

Let me explain...

The Jubilee is a Jewish economic tradition. It is part of the Old Testament. You'll find it described in the Book of Leviticus, Chapter 25. The idea was simple. At the end of 49 years, all debts would be wiped out and collateral property returned.

It was a way of completely "resetting" the financial order... of making sure the wealthy didn't become too dominant... of making sure the economy didn't collapse... of making sure there was never a violent revolution.

You see, economies collapse when debt-service costs grow faster than income for a long time – usually 50 years or more. Jubilees aren't normal default cycles. They are far different... These are debt-fueled revolutions.

What happens is that debt builds and builds. Once debt-service costs start growing faster than the economy, the total debt is never reduced. Sooner or later, debt begins to grow geometrically, far faster than income. And then... it simply can't be managed. That's when the crisis hits.

These debt revolutions are characterized by the inability of the debt burden to be reduced in "normal" ways. In a normal cycle, deleveraging reduces debt burdens. And this happens through some combination of reduced spending (to pay off debt), defaults (where assets are redistributed among creditors), and increased money supply (to prevent a deflationary spiral and stoke economic growth).

But in a debt revolution, those normal measures don't work. Austerity causes a big reduction in economic growth. Spending slows and the economy declines faster than debt can be reduced.

Likewise, the debt burdens can be so big that defaults don't work because the collateral won't come close to covering the debt. (Think about General Motors' bankruptcy. The government put an additional $50 billion into the company, and it still couldn't pay its creditors.)

And sometimes, even extreme amounts of money printing don't work because interest costs increase more than inflation, causing the debt burden to continually grow faster than the economy.

What happens in these situations?

When deleveraging doesn't work, the debt burden grows and grows. It begins to weigh heavier and heavier across the poorest segments of society. It becomes life-choking. It leads to despair. To depression. To violence. And to revolution.

The federal debt burden has been growing uncontrollably for the last decade. Since 2008, total U.S. federal debt has more than doubled. That is, our government has borrowed more money in the last 10 years than it borrowed in the prior 231 years of its existence, combined.

Yes, in terms of debt to gross domestic product (GDP), government borrowing was larger during the Civil War and World War II. That's true. But it's also irrelevant...

What really matters is that it's not only the government's debt that continues to grow uncontrollably.

What really matters is that our country's total debt load (household, corporate, and government) continues to grow. Even after the crisis of 2008. Even with $4 trillion in new money. Even with the huge number of mortgage defaults (over $1 trillion in losses).

What really matters is that now, more so than ever before, the burden of these debts is falling most heavily on the poorest members of our society – the people most likely to be radicalized. The people most likely to be violent. The people most likely to declare a Jubilee.

Most Americans believe the 2008-2011 financial crisis solved our debt problem...

We all know someone who defaulted on his mortgage and hasn't been able to borrow money since. Most of us believe that solved the problem... that everything is fine now. (Well, except for the government's debt... But that's a different kind of problem.)

The facts tell a different story.

U.S. total debt (household, corporate, and government) hasn't declined since 2008.

Federal debt only declined in one quarter (first quarter 2017, -2.6%) since 2008. Household debt only declined twice (2010 and 2011 by less than 1%). And corporate debt has declined twice, too (-4% in 2009, less than 1% in 2010).

As of 2017, total debt is growing at almost 4% a year. Since 2008, our economy has grown an average 2.9% a year. **That means, once again, our debts are growing much faster than our economy**.

Our economy did not deleverage. The "normal" methods of reducing our country's debt burdens *did not work*.

Economists will be quick to tell you that this doesn't really matter because *debt service* burdens fell. That has allowed disposable income to rise and led to "solid" economic growth that, eventually, will allow these debts to be repaid.

Please remember this idea: **It is because debt service obligations have fallen (relative to GDP) that our economy recovered, not because of any reduction in debt load.**

Interest rates have fallen dramatically over the past eight years. Yields on corporate junk bonds have never been lower. Same with yields on government debt. Same with most mortgage loans. These huge reductions in borrowing costs allowed the economy to continue growing despite the lack of any deleveraging and the continued growth of our debt burden.

These massive reductions in interest rates were caused by the Federal Reserve's actions... which are now being reversed.

There's another problem that most people haven't figured out yet...

Most of the household credit growth over the last few years wasn't in mortgages, which are normally safe loans. They're well collateralized. And most people who buy a house have the income required to support the loan. *The new debt has been highly concentrated in the poorest segments of our society.*

Credit Suisse Chief Global Strategist Jonathan Wilmot published some debt research that looked at debt-to-income ratios across different segments of the population. In the late 1980s, the 20% of Americans with the least amount of income held little debt, when measured against their income levels. Today, however, this segment of the population is the most in debt when measured against income.

The poorest Americans now hold debts in excess of 250% of their incomes, or about five times more debt than the wealthiest 20%.

This massive change in the character of our household debts came about because of "innovations" in lending – like subprime auto loans, pay day lenders, and, most important, student loans.

In November 2017, total household debt is almost $13 trillion. That's higher than the previous all-time high of $12.6 trillion, set in the third quarter of 2008 – immediately prior to the last crisis.

And what's most important to understand is that the cost of this debt burden has been artificially reduced since 2009 by the Fed. These costs – not just the normal debt service, but also the cost of defaults – are about to soar.

More than 10% of these loans are student loans ($1.5 trillion outstanding). Most were made to poor people against zero collateral, where there isn't any legal process to deal with defaults. This is a *serious economic problem* that will transform into a serious political problem because we have no economic or legal way to deal with these debts.

In other words... this massive debt bubble has mostly been created by the 44 million Americans who have student loans. These are the people in our society who are the least able to manage their debts. They are the most likely to default.

In 2016, no payments were made by more than 4 million borrowers against a total of $137 billion in outstanding student loans. **This represents a 14% *annual* increase in the default rate from 2015. On average, 3,000 new people default on their student loans each day.**

And yet... the issuance of these bad debts continues to soar. Since 2013, the average balance of all student borrowers has increased by 17% to more than $30,000.

What do you think happens next?

What happens when the least educated, least "vested," and most violent members of your society (unmarried men in their 20s) make up the largest demographic block... and have the largest debts (relative to income) with zero ability to pay back these debts or discharge them through bankruptcy?

Forty-four million people carry a student loan. Most of them can't afford these loans. Nor can they default. They can't restructure. They're stuck – many with $100,000 loans that absorb more than 100% of their disposable income.

What do you think they are going to do?

All they can do is fight...

When you watch the news and you see people rioting about race in Charlottesville, Virginia... when you see the inner cities burning in Baltimore, Maryland... when you see more and more radicalized politics – like resurgent neo-Nazi groups, the rise of Black Lives Matter protests, and college students embracing violence to protest at any conservative speaker – what you're really seeing is the beginning of the Jubilee.

These protests may nominally be about race. Or about Donald Trump. But what they are really about is hopelessness. What they are really about is economics.

The poor – and especially the young and poor in our country – have no hope of being able to afford the American dream. Not when median incomes are $60,000 and the average college debt is more than $30,000. Not when the average cost of a house is more than $250,000 and a decent apartment is unaffordable for most college graduates.

The Jubilee has started in America. You haven't seen it yet. But it's there.

The idea is actively being pushed by some of the most influential "progressive" economists and academics...

London School of Economics Professor David Graeber wrote an entire book on the subject and said...

> We are long overdue for some kind of Biblical-style Jubilee... it would relieve so much genuine human suffering.

The national affairs correspondent for *The Nation* said we should...

> Think Jubilee, American Style... because it combines a sense of social justice with old-fashioned common sense.

Paul Kedrosky, a senior fellow at the Kaufman Foundation (a liberal think tank), said...

> We need a fresh start, and we need it now... we need... a Jubilee.

Economist and author Professor Steve Keen said...

> It is incumbent for society to reduce the debt burden sooner rather than later... So a *prima facie* alternative to 15 years of deleveraging is an old-fashioned debt Jubilee.

The list goes on and on...

Harvard economist Carmen Reinhart has called for a Debt Jubilee. So have financial pundits such as Barry Ritholtz and Chris Whalen. So has renowned economist Stephen Roach of Yale University.

In Congress, more than a half-dozen Jubilee-style laws have already been proposed, by folks such as Representative Kathy Castor and Senator Bill Nelson from Florida.

Representative Castor says getting rid of debts will "spur job growth, strengthen our economy, and guarantee a bright and boundless future for our country."

Mark Zuckerberg (founder of Facebook) recently toured all 50 states. His message: We should forgive all student loans and offer a guaranteed income to every American. Likewise, both the Hillary Clinton and Bernie Sanders campaigns pledged to forgive student loans and make college "free."

That's the fourth way to deleverage an economy.

I already mentioned the three normal ways: austerity... default... and money printing. You can also redistribute the wealth. That's the Jubilee.

We've been trying the first three ways for almost 10 years. They haven't worked, at all. Instead, the debt burden has only grown larger, and it has grown fastest on the backs of the poorest members of our society. This does not bode well for the stability of our country.

Think about it... Most of the voting households in our country can't handle a $400 emergency. Millions and millions of them have a debt burden they can't afford. So out of the four ways to reduce our economy's debt burden, which do you think we're going to try next?

It's a Jubilee. And just like Shirley Jackson's lottery, it's likely to be incredibly violent... with the young brutally taking from the old.

President Trump comes up for re-election in 2020. That's 49 years since the last Jubilee in America, in 1971. That's when Nixon repudiated our government's debt by abandoning the Bretton Woods gold-standard system and telling our creditors, who had been promised payment in gold, to "go pound sand."

Since then, total debt in America has soared from around 100% of GDP to close to 400% of GDP. You may remember the 1970s. The violent protests. The soaring inflation. The feeling that the country was coming apart at the seams.

Well, this time will be about four times worse.

The Jubilee is coming. And you'd better get ready for it.

Part I

What Is the American Debt Jubilee?

– Chapter 1 –

A Major Jubilee Is Coming to America

If you study American history, you'll see that Debt Jubilees occur only in a unique type of extreme political environment.

After all, a Jubilee is a radical measure.

The government essentially steals money from one group and hands it to another.

In order for this to occur, four elements must be in place...

1. The **wealth gap** must be getting dramatically bigger.

2. There must be **cultural threats** from those with different values or from outsiders (in other words, minority populations and immigrants).

3. The **government must be ineffective** at providing solutions.

4. And there must be **growing anger toward the "elites."**

Sounds familiar, doesn't it?

We have the largest gap ever between the rich and poor...

We have huge increases in violent protests about immigration and race...

We have a completely ineffective government...

And we have extreme animosity toward the "elites" from both the left and right.

Check... check... check... and check.

There's actually a name for this type of political and social phenomenon. It's called "Populism." And it emerges every 30 to 40 years.

Populist movements are characterized by extreme anger at the government, at the wealthy, at the establishments, and at "newcomers" and minorities.

As the director of an Alabama group that tracks violence and hate crimes around the country told *Newsweek* in June 2017: "There has been a massive explosion of violence across the country."

I'm sure you've seen this yourself.

The hatred and anger is like nothing I've witnessed in my lifetime. And it's coming from all sides. A member of my staff went to a book reading in Baltimore by one of the most famous left-wing authors in the country.

The author told the crowd that he wished he could go back in time and smother Donald Trump in his crib as a baby... or convince Trump's mother to have an abortion.

This epitomizes the political and social environment in America today.

From the protests and marches... to the refusals to stand during the national anthem...

From Black Lives Matter to the anti-immigration movements... to the rejuvenation of White Supremacists... to the tripling of membership in the Democratic Socialists of America.

It's clear we are in the middle of an extreme "Populist" period in America.

Ray Dalio, one of the richest men in America, studied the political environments of the past 100 years and concluded in March 2017...

> The last time that it [Populism] existed as a major force in the world was in the 1930s, when most countries became Populist. Over the last year, it has again emerged as a major force.

Look at this chart. The big spikes show when Populist politicians got the most votes in America and abroad...

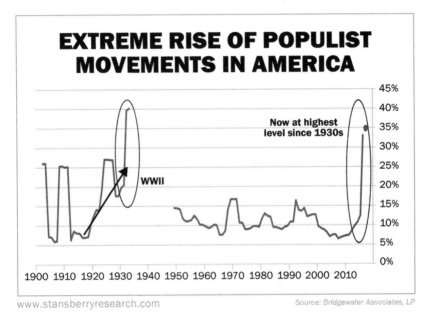

EXTREME RISE OF POPULIST MOVEMENTS IN AMERICA

Now at highest level since 1930s

WWII

www.stansberryresearch.com   Source: *Bridgewater Associates, LP*

So what does this all mean?

It proves that what we're experiencing today is eerily similar to what happened in the 1930s... right before the biggest and most radical Debt Jubilee in American history.

The economic comparison is stunning.

Interest rates hit zero leading up to each of these periods...

Source: Bridgewater Associates, LP

The government went into mega money-printing mode during both periods...

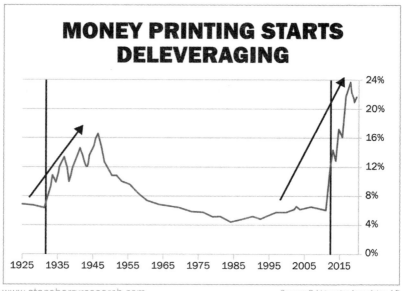

Source: Bridgewater Associates, LP

Printing money caused the stock market and other risky assets to boom during both periods... boosting the wealth of the rich, but doing nothing for the poor...

Dow Jones Industrial Average

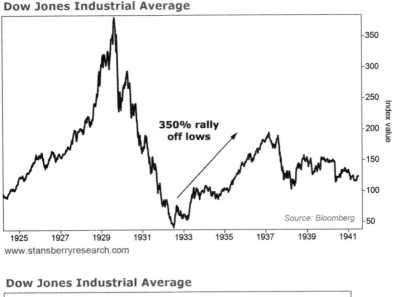

www.stansberryresearch.com

Dow Jones Industrial Average

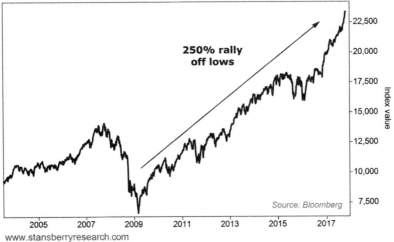

www.stansberryresearch.com

During the 1930s, just like today, the wealthy acquired a much higher than normal percentage of our nation's wealth...

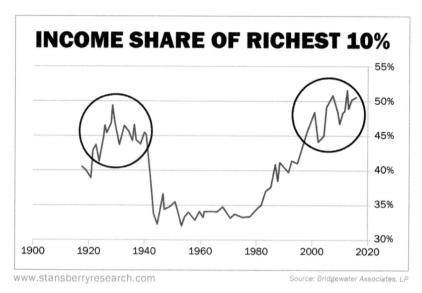

 Source: Bridgewater Associates, LP

And in both the 1930s and today, the percentage of the population who were foreign born was higher than normal... causing animosity among the "common man."

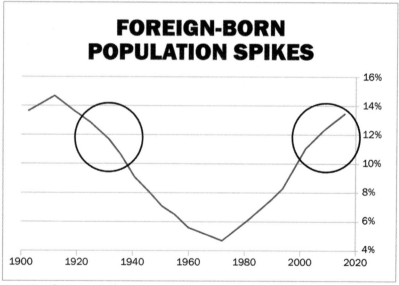

 Source: Bridgewater Associates, LP

Just like today, the economic conditions of the 1930s caused extreme income inequality.

Back then, the top 10% earned 45% of all income (compared with 50% today) and owned 85% of the wealth (compared with 75% today).

Even the political characters are the same...

The 1930s saw a popular socialist presidential candidate just like we had in 2016. Huey Long was a former governor of Louisiana and a U.S. senator. He proposed an income cap at $1 million... a 30-hour federal work week... and 100% income taxes at the highest level.

Long even established 27,000 "Share Our Wealth" clubs around the country and had a radio show that was listened to by one in five Americans.

So where did this all lead? It led to America's most dramatic Debt Jubilee to date...

How Americans Lost 69% of Their Savings

In 1933 – in order to deal with mounting debts and print money to pay for dozens of new social programs – President Roosevelt made two extraordinary changes to the financial system.

First, he closed banks for four days and forced Americans to turn in each ounce of gold they owned for $20.67 in paper money.

Then the government raised the price of gold, wiping out 69% of the savings of anyone who followed these rules.

You're probably familiar with that part of the story.

But that was only the beginning...

Roosevelt also eliminated the "Gold Clause" in all contracts, including loans, bonds, and other financial instruments.

You see, at the time, people were worried the government might inflate away the value of their money.

So they added a Gold Clause, which said repayments could be required to be made in gold.

7

These Gold Clauses were not in federal loans, bank deposits, insurance contracts, and other private agreements.

When Roosevelt outlawed the Gold Clause, he stole billions from investors. In fact, a Harvard paper estimates this rule **took $700 million a year** from private investors who bought government bonds.

Billions more were stolen from folks who lost money from the elimination of the Gold Clause in private contracts, bank accounts, and insurance deals.

Eliminating the Gold Clause was so controversial, investors sued the government. The case went to the Supreme Court.

Roosevelt was terrified his Debt Jubilee would be overturned. He even drafted a speech saying he would ignore the court if it ruled against him.

But his political pressure worked, and the court ruled 5-4 in Roosevelt's favor.

Of course, there were consequences...

Tens of millions of Americans lost massive amounts of their savings. And after booming, the stock market soon fell 50% in a single year.

Investor confidence was crushed. Supreme Court Justice Harlan Fiske Stone vowed he would never buy another federal bond.

We had another Debt Jubilee in America about 40 years later...

Starting in the late 1960s, we saw another Populist uprising... a combination of economic and social upheaval.

If you're old enough to remember, think about the anger and resentment of the 1960s.

The Black Panthers' slogan was: "Power to the People." The idols of the day were people like Latin-American guerrilla leader Che Guevara, Malcolm X, and Muhammad Ali.

All over the country, there was one clash after another...

Small farmers fought banks and railroads... union workers battled their bosses and federal judges. On college campuses, students fought anyone with authority. Election rallies routinely ended in violence.

Things were so bad, Lyndon Johnson decided not to run for re-election. Martin Luther King, Jr. and Robert Kennedy were assassinated.

In 1968 alone, there were violent uprisings in more than 120 U.S. cities.

A few miles from where my company is headquartered today, thousands of National Guard troops and 500 state police officers were brought in to quell the violence and looting.

At the same time, a major financial crisis was brewing...

The government had borrowed extraordinary sums, and we were having a hard time repaying creditors.

That's because at the time, every dollar was required to be backed by $0.25 worth of gold. So the government couldn't print unlimited amounts of money out of thin air.

Also, foreign creditors who owned U.S. government bonds were allowed to collect repayments in gold bullion instead of dollars... so our gold reserves were quickly disappearing.

Get this: Between 1958 to 1968, 52% of America's gold reserves left the country in the form of repayments for our debts.

The government was scared. It knew there was only one way out... another Debt Jubilee.

First, we eliminated the 25% gold backing of every dollar.

Then, in 1971, President Nixon completely defaulted on our promise to pay gold for dollars to our foreign creditors.

Once again, the government simply wiped the slate clean.

No one could redeem dollars for gold any longer.

This allowed the Fed to print as much money as it needed to make payments on our debts.

But once again, there were consequences...

In the 1970s, the U.S. dollar lost 30% of its value over a several-year period. Inflation more than doubled. And the stock market fell 48% in less than two years.

Unemployment was around 10%. And, believe it or not, the Federal government got so desperate that it issued "Carter Bonds" *denominated in Swiss francs because the U.S. dollar could no longer be trusted.*

That brings us to today.

Once again, the stage is set for America's next Debt Jubilee.

We are living in a world of two different Americas. For the wealthiest 40% of the population, life is good. Asset prices are rising... and wages are finally starting to increase.

For everyone else, life is getting worse...

For the bottom 60% of America, consumer debt is high and wages are stagnant. Most of these folks would have difficulty raising even a few hundred dollars for an emergency. These folks have less than $20,000 on average saved for retirement. Physical and mental health is deteriorating. And death rates are soaring. Premature deaths are up by 20% since 2000.

As Bridgewater Associates wrote in a 2017 report...

> The biggest contributors to that change are an increase in deaths by drugs/poisoning (up two times since 2000) and an increase in suicides (up over 50% since 2000).

That is the definition of hopelessness.

And it's why the inevitable Jubilee in America is already underway...

The concept of a Jubilee comes from the Bible (The Old Testament), the Book of Leviticus, Chapter 25.

A Jubilee in the Jewish tradition was said to occur roughly every 50 years. It was a time for total forgiveness of debt and the freeing of slaves.

Pope Boniface VIII proclaimed the first Christian Jubilee in 1300. And rulers throughout history have occasionally used a Jubilee to reset the financial system – especially when the poorest citizens are threatening revolt.

Today, the vast majority of America is in bad shape. And the poorest citizens are calling for a radical solution...

But this Jubilee will be different from the 1933 and 1971 ones we've discussed.

The federal government is free to print all the money it needs to pay government debts. Private households are different.

The only ways out of private debt are to pay it, to default, or to have it forgiven with a Debt Jubilee.

Today, America's low-income households don't have the funds to service the money they owe. It's mathematically impossible. And politicians will never allow tens of millions of our poorest citizens to go bankrupt.

So the only solution left is a Debt Jubilee.

It will be similar to the one that took place in 1841 in America...

Back then, the laws were temporarily changed, so debtors could be discharged of their debts – without the consent of the creditors. Over a period of 13 months, more than 40,000 people wiped away their debts before the act was rescinded.

Today, it will be tens of millions of people and trillions of dollars.

And once again, there will be consequences...

Millions of investors, pensioners, insurance customers, and creditors will lose a fortune. Stocks will collapse. Dozens of companies will go bankrupt.

I'm not saying this to scare you. This is simply the reality we face.

In this book, we'll walk you through the critical information you need to know to keep your money safe during the next Debt Jubilee.

We'll look at the main investments you should own and the ones you should avoid. We'll discuss the largest part of wealth that most Americans overlook – but that could prevent your entire retirement nest egg from disappearing. And we'll share our crash course on how to become a better investor in the process.

The Jubilee is already starting. Protect your financial accounts. Get out of the common investments that are most likely to get crushed. Focus on ways to profit while everyone else loses their shirt.

And learn all you can about the corruptions destroying America...

— Chapter 2 —

The Corruption of Politics

It is routinely alleged in national political debates that something is fundamentally unfair and un-American about the huge wealth gap between the poorest and the wealthiest Americans.

Some politicians like to argue that the poor never have a real shot at the American dream. So as a nation, we owe them more and more of our resources to correct this injustice. Most important, *they claim only the government has the resources to correct this inequality.*

These are dangerous notions...

They promote a sense of entitlement. The American idea of entitlement argues that because you were born into a rich society, other people owe you something. The idea has become pervasive in our culture. It underlies the basic assumptions behind the idea of a wealth gap.

Implicit is the assumption that successful Americans haven't rightfully earned their wealth... that in one way or another, they've taken advantage of the society and have an obligation to "give back" what they've "taken."

As you'll see, the idea of entitlement lies at the root of many of our most serious cultural problems.

The more obvious problem is the idea that the government is responsible for fixing the "wealth gap." But the government has proven wholly ineffective at dealing with poverty in America. The data is conclusive that government efforts are far more likely to be the cause of the wealth gap than the solution.

This leads to one of the core facets of our problem: **Government doesn't produce anything**. Anything it gives to one person or group, it must first take from someone else. It sucks capital out of the productive economy and uses it for activities that are largely unproductive.

The crisis we face is the inevitable result of the ways the government goes about taking the resources it has promised.

Let's use Detroit as an example...

In 1961, Detroit elected Democrat Jerome Cavanagh as mayor.

He won election by promising to give Detroit's African American population the civil rights they deserved. But Cavanagh didn't stop there. Seeing the political advantage of serving this community's interests, he did all he could to bring government benefits and government spending to Detroit's black community.

Mayor Cavanagh modeled development in Detroit after Soviet efforts to rebuild whole urban areas in Eastern Europe. The program attempted to turn a nine-square-mile section of the city (with 134,000 inhabitants) into a "Model City."

To help finance the effort, Cavanagh pushed a new income tax through the state legislature and a "commuter tax" on city workers. He promised the residents of the Model City... most of whom were poor and black... benefits that would be paid for by the rich. He bought the votes of the city's residents with taxes they didn't have to pay.

More than $490 million (almost $3.7 billion in today's dollars) was spent on the program. The feds and Democratic city mayors were soon telling people where to live, what to build, and what businesses to open or close. In return, the people received cash, training, education, and health care.

But they didn't like being told what to do or how to live. The Model City program was a disaster. Within five years, it had helped trigger a complete breakdown of civil order. The city's population began to rapidly decline.

On July 23, 1967, police attempted to break up a notorious after-hours club that featured gambling and prostitution in the heart of the new Model City. Many of these clubs had been in operation since Prohibition. The community tolerated these establishments – but the city's political leadership didn't want them in the new Model City area.

On this particular night, at this particular club, the community was celebrating the return of two Vietnam War veterans. More than 80 people had packed into the club. The police decided to arrest everyone present, including the two war vets. This outraged the entire neighborhood, which began to riot. The scene turned into the worst race riot of the 1960s.

The violence killed more than 40 people and left more than 5,000 people homeless. One of the first stores to be looted was a black-owned pharmacy. The largest black-owned clothing store in the city was also burned to the ground. Cavanagh did nothing to stop the riots. (He claimed a large police presence would make matters worse.) Five days later, President Johnson sent in two divisions of paratroopers to put down the violence.

The situation destabilized the entire city. Most of the people who could afford to leave did. Over the next 18 months, 140,000 upper- and middle-class residents – almost all of them white – left the city.

And so, you might ask... after five years of centralized planning, higher taxes, and a fleeing population... what did the government decide to do with its grand experiment?

It expanded the Model City program with 1974's Community Development Block Grant Program.

The subsequent failure of this program and many after it has decimated Detroit's economy and culture. Almost nothing is left of what was the capital of America's industrial heartland. Total vacant land in Detroit now occupies an area the size of Boston.

None of this is surprising. It's exactly what you'd expect to see given the implementation of a socialist scheme like the Model City program.

Always remember... **the government has to take resources from someone before it can dole them out to others**. This act of taking destroys an economy. The more you take from the productive members of society, the less productive they become. That's the primary lesson of the history of socialism. Yet many of our political leaders seem oblivious to this iron law of human nature.

So... how does the government go about taking the resources it has promised to distribute?

The first and most obvious way – **taxes**.

You don't need me to tell you, our politicians have taken full advantage of their power to tax. But we're reaching their limits... Taxes can no longer be raised without people fleeing states. This has happened in several places – California, New Jersey, and New York, to name a few.

In Maryland – where my company is headquartered – the Democratic state government couldn't balance the budget in 2009, so it decided to double the income tax rate on citizens with more than $1 million in annual income. The editorial board at the *Baltimore Sun* newspaper happily praised the measure and predicted Maryland's top earners would "grin and bear it"... What a bunch of fools.

Instead, the rich left. The number of million-dollar incomes in the state of Maryland declined by more than 30%. Rather than gaining the predicted $106 million in income from these filers, Maryland collected $100 million _less_ than it did the year before.

It's good politics to promise the voters that only the rich will pay. But it's terrible economics, because it never works out the way the government plans.

Now take a look at the next chart... You'll see that in 1950, the government only represented 23% of our country's GDP.

By 2016, that government slice was much bigger – 36%.

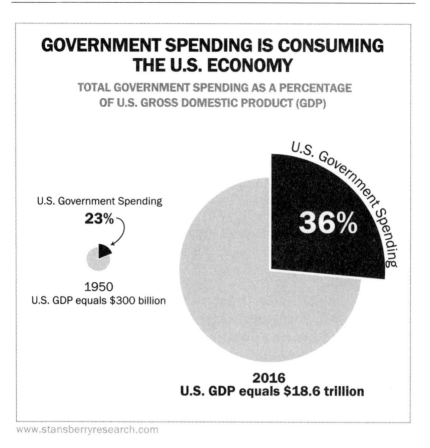

GOVERNMENT SPENDING IS CONSUMING THE U.S. ECONOMY

TOTAL GOVERNMENT SPENDING AS A PERCENTAGE OF U.S. GROSS DOMESTIC PRODUCT (GDP)

U.S. Government Spending

23%

1950
U.S. GDP equals $300 billion

U.S. Government Spending

36%

**2016
U.S. GDP equals $18.6 trillion**

www.stansberryresearch.com

A huge portion of that pie comes directly from income taxes. But those taxes aren't evenly distributed across the whole country. The burden for an overwhelming amount of the taxes the government collects falls on just a few people.

The Tax Policy Center estimates that 45% of U.S. households will not pay federal income taxes for 2017.

And the top 25% of our country's earners pay nearly 90% of all income taxes collected.

This leads the 45% of Americans who don't pay federal income taxes to believe the government doesn't cost them anything.

They are dead wrong.

Everyone is paying for the government whether they realize it or not. The 36% of GDP that the government consumes comes out of everyone's pockets.

The tax revenue may come from the rich. But this capital would otherwise be used to start new businesses, create jobs, and invest in innovation.

Even those who do not pay taxes lose out on what would have been created by the existence of that money in the productive economy.

It also reduces the market's incentives for entrepreneurs. **The more you take from the productive members of society, the less productive they become**. That's the primary lesson of the history of socialism.

Another way the government takes resources from the productive members of society and doles it out to everyone else is by **simply changing the laws via a Jubilee**.

Right now, it's impossible to know which mechanism the government will use to implement the Jubilee.

It could confiscate 25% of every American's 401(k). There's roughly $5 trillion available in these accounts.

It could do another round of quantitative easing, purchasing consumer debt instead of Treasurys.

Or it could simply force creditors to take the losses. This happened in Croatia... In 2015, the government erased more than $20 million in debts for 60,000 people. This was money owed to banks, telecom operators, municipal authorities, and utility companies. No one was refunded for their losses. The stock market fell significantly over the next year.

America's Jubilee would likely be 100,000-times higher than what we saw in Croatia (around $2 trillion compared with $20 million).

Rob Johnson, a former banker, who runs the Institute of New Economic Thinking, explained how he'd like to see the upcoming Jubilee implemented...

You call a month-long bank holiday for the 20 largest banks, and that holds everything in place while the regulators mark down the assets and see how everybody's losses will affect everyone else.

Then you wipe out stockholders, wipe out management, possibly some of the unsecured debt... Once everybody has taken their hit and you've wiped out existing stockholders, then the government comes in and properly, transparently recapitalizes all of them. As these new institutions gain a footing, eventually they can be sold back to the private market.

The point is, we don't know exactly how it will be done. But through one mechanism or another, the Fed will wipe out trillions of dollars in bad debt.

Car companies, homebuilders, credit card companies, insurance firms, banks, other lending institutions, and any business operating with leverage will take a huge hit. Stocks will fall considerably. Banks will close. There will be trillions in losses.

At the end of the day, the losses at an institution like Wells Fargo could be enough to start a bank run. And once a bank run starts, look out. It's nearly impossible to stop.

— Chapter 3 —

The Corruption of Debt

Again, the only way government can give away something is by first taking it from someone else. This is critical. The government taking what it wants is exactly what has created the crisis we face.

Taxes are the most obvious way the government takes what it wants to redistribute. But as I said, our government is reaching the limits of what it can generate from new or higher taxes. When the government realizes it can't take any more from you through taxes, it uses debt to take from your children and grandchildren.

And our government has taken advantage of that option to a historic degree...

As of November 2017, the U.S. government owes more than $20 trillion. The number is so large, it's meaningless. No one can comprehend how much money $20 trillion really is. A better way to think about it is each American taxpayer owes roughly $165,000. That's like a whole additional mortgage for most people.

A 2014 Harvard study put it in this way:

> If the federal government spent its yearly revenues exclusively on debt reduction and ceased all of its operations, it would take three of four years to pay down the debt. Or, the government could pay down the debt in one blow if it simply took more than $52,000 from every person living in the U.S., including children, the elderly, and the unemployed. If this one-time "debt reduction fee" were levied only on those in the workforce, the cost would be over $106,000 per person.

And it's not just the federal government that has become addicted to debt. If you add up all of our government, corporate, and consumer debt, America owes roughly $67 trillion.

As the next chart shows... that adds up to about $808,000 per American household.

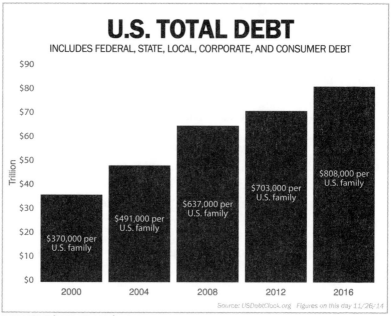

U.S. TOTAL DEBT

INCLUDES FEDERAL, STATE, LOCAL, CORPORATE, AND CONSUMER DEBT

Source: USDebtClock.org Figures on this day 11/26/14

www.stansberryresearch.com

This massive amount of national debt cannot be financed at any real rate of interest.

If the government had to pay even 6% interest on its debt, it would cost roughly $1.2 trillion a year. And that's just to pay the interest on the debt. The entire government brings in about $3.6 trillion a year in taxes.

The next chart shows what would happen in that scenario...

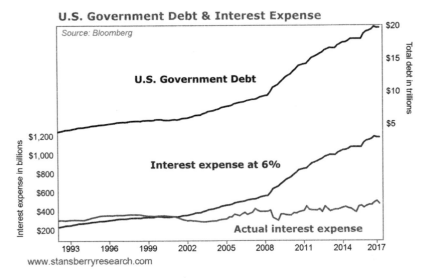

U.S. Government Debt & Interest Expense

Source: Bloomberg

U.S. Government Debt

Interest expense at 6%

Actual interest expense

www.stansberryresearch.com

This debt addiction has filtered into three critical areas of the economy. Instead of learning from the mistakes that crippled our economy in 2009 when the mortgage bubble burst, we have created three new bubbles that could soon blow up...

The largest threat is the U.S. corporate bond market, particularly junk bonds.

When this crash occurs, it will be the largest destruction of wealth in history. There has never been a bigger bubble in U.S. bonds.

How do I know? It's simple. Historically, junk bonds (aka high-yield bonds issued by less creditworthy companies) have never yielded less than 5% annually. But they hit that low in mid-2014, and in November 2017, they were up to about 5.7%.

Likewise, in 2014, the difference between the yields on junk bonds and the yields on investment-grade bonds had almost never been smaller. That means credit was more available than almost ever before for small, less-than-investment-grade firms. The last time credit was that widely available – and at such low costs – was in 2007. And that ended badly.

Throughout 2015, the spread between low-quality corporate bonds and high-quality corporate bonds began rising. That indicated a growing fear in the market as people reduced the amount of risk in their portfolios and shifted to higher-quality and higher-rated assets.

During the first half of 2017, the high-yield spread again declined... indicating complacency in the high-yield (aka "junk") debt market. But it won't last. It never does.

The coming collapse in the bond market will be far worse than it was last time, too. The Federal Reserve's twin policies of keeping interest rates near zero and buying tens of billions of dollars in Treasury securities and mortgage-backed debt have driven the huge bull market in bonds. As the Fed buys bonds, it pushes bond rates down and forces the other buyers of bonds to buy riskier debt that historically offers much higher yields.

I believe we'll see a real panic in the corporate bond market at some point soon. I expect the average price of non-investment-grade debt (aka junk bonds) to fall 50%. Investment-grade bonds will fall substantially, too. (I'd estimate something around 25%.) This is going to wipe out a huge amount of capital... and believe me... it's almost 100% guaranteed to happen.

Junk-bond guru Martin Fridson has projected $1.6 trillion of bonds and loans will default. That means three times as many debt issuers will default than the last recession.

This would have already happened, according to Fridson, but the government has kept interest rates artificially low, making it possible for many at-risk debt-issuers to refinance their debt at a lower interest rate. This delayed an inevitable wave of defaults in the junk-bond industry, but only temporarily. But the government cannot keep interest rates low forever...

Meanwhile, **student debt is forming another looming bubble**.

Over the past 10 years, students (most of whom have virtually no income) have racked up *enormous* debts. As of 2017, student debt totals more than **$1.5 trillion – the second-largest source of household debt after home mortgages**.

Incredibly, that's what our entire federal government owed a little more than 30 years ago. Virtually all of this money was borrowed in only the last 10 years.

The average college student graduates with more than $30,000 in debt... and by his late 20s has racked up more than $6,000 in credit card debt. Meanwhile, median earnings for Americans aged 25-34 equals $36,000-$40,000.

Can you imagine starting out your adult life with a personal debt-to-income level at close to 100%? What does this say about the state of our economy? What does this say about the state of our culture?

All the signs show that the debt piled on our youth will become another catastrophic bubble in the American economy.

Student debt is at record levels. Total indebtedness doubled from 2009 to 2016. The burden is causing borrowers to cut spending and other forms of borrowing. About one in every four borrowers is delinquent or in default. And 42% of federally owned student loans aren't being repaid as expected or on time.

Jim Rickards, the author of *Currency Wars,* calls the student debt market the "next sub-prime crisis."

According to the *Wall Street Journal,* **33%** of student loans are held by subprime borrowers – the riskiest folks.

What does it say about our economy when the youth have become saddled with so much debt that one-third of college graduates will likely default on their loans?

And it's not just college kids who have buried themselves in debt...

U.S. consumers now owe more than $1 trillion on their credit cards. These debts carry interest rates as high as 28% annually.

The third subprime lending bubble poised to cripple the economy is the automotive sector. Most people have no idea how pervasive subprime loans have become in auto lending.

As with mortgage lending, car lending used to be a simple and safe business. Local and regional banks (or finance companies) would provide loans to customers with good credit and a substantial down payment.

The term of the loan didn't exceed the useful life of the car. Under these conditions, auto loans were extremely low-risk. Losses on auto loans have historically been extremely low – less than 2%. Auto loans even performed well in the Great Depression.

Then things got out of control in 2011, after Wall Street firms started buying up auto-lending groups. They changed the terms: extending auto loans up to 84 months (seven years), lowering the down payments (on leases they're next to nothing), and radically lowering the credit scores required to qualify.

Now, more people than ever before are borrowing money to buy cars. Americans now owe more than $1 trillion for auto loans. More than 40% of the adult population has an auto loan, and some of the rates are as high as 20%.

Unbelievably, 37% of this debt is owed by either non-prime, sub-prime, or deep sub-prime credits.

We've also seen a big uptick in the amount of subprime auto loans that are being securitized and sold to other investors. These securitizations move credit risk away from the car companies and finance companies and onto investors – the same thing that happened in the housing bubble.

As we know from the recent housing bust... when subprime lending goes too far and becomes too large a percentage of total lending, it can cause overall credit quality to collapse. In the car business, that could cause huge problems going forward, problems big enough to harm our entire economy.

The debt situation in this country has gotten so bad, 73% of Americans now die in debt... leaving behind an average total of more than $60,000.

This debt will create a depression that will be worse than it was in 2008. This time, the government has allowed massive amounts of debt to be piled on the weakest in our society. **The poor – and**

especially the young and poor in our country – have no hope of being able to afford the American dream anymore.

When this bubble breaks, it will be an entire generation of young Americans who will suffer.

Here's what's critical to understand: This kind of debt burden for the poorest Americans is new. The debt load for the poorest 20% of Americans is up nearly 300% in the past 20 years.

Debts of this magnitude cannot be financed normally. Debts that can't be paid won't be paid. In other words: It's not just the size of Americans' debts that's the problem. *It's who owes the money that's the bigger concern.*

When the rich – a tiny percentage of the population – get in trouble with debt, it's an economic problem. But when the poor and middle class get in trouble with debt – a huge percentage of the population – it's a political problem.

That's what makes a national Debt Jubilee inevitable.

The United States has become the largest debtor in human history. It's disgusting that we would leave a burden like this for our children and grandchildren.

The obvious question is: ***Why on Earth did so many people borrow so much money they have no hope of ever repaying?***

You might assume it stems from a lack of personal responsibility or a decline in moral standards in recent years. And that did play a role... There is always a segment of society that wants something for nothing.

But this doesn't explain how this problem could grow so large.

The real reason is something else: The final corruption of America...

Ignore for a moment how impossible it is for us to pay off the debts we have accumulated. We are fast approaching the point where the government cannot even afford to pay the interest on the debt.

And that leaves it with one last tool to perpetuate its power...

— Chapter 4 —

The Corruption of Currency

When the government taps out its ability to increase its tax revenue and its debts become too mountainous to maintain... it has one last way it can take what it needs. And it may be the most insidious.

It can print the dollars it needs to pay for what it wants.

This is a relatively new phenomenon for the U.S. government. Throughout most of our history, one thing kept our government from printing all the dollars it wanted – gold. Until the mid-20th century, the dollar represented an explicit promise. It represented one small claim on the U.S. government's gold reserve. And the size of the reserve limited the dollars available for circulation.

But in 1971, Nixon severed the U.S. dollar's last tie to gold. From then on, we were free to take on as much debt as the world would lend us... and print as much money as we needed to finance it.

Since the 2008-2009 financial crisis, the Federal Reserve has largely kept the printing presses running full-tilt. Its quantitative easing policies (printing billions of dollars and using them to buy Treasury securities and mortgage-backed debt) have caused the volume of currency to balloon.

The Federal Reserve's balance sheet – which represents the total amount of currency in circulation or in a central bank's reserves – has blown up from $1.1 trillion in 2008 to nearly $4 trillion in 2017.

Federal Reserve Monetary Base

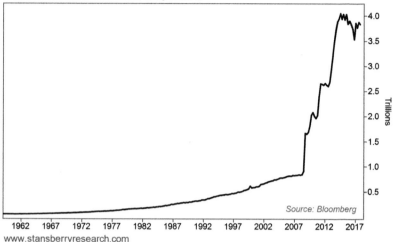

Source: Bloomberg

www.stansberryresearch.com

Not many people understand the fallacy of these actions or their inevitable failure. The great advantage of paper money is supposed to be its flexibility. You can, in theory, print more of it when you need it to facilitate economic growth or forestall a crisis. But it doesn't really work.

Printing money doesn't create wealth or stimulate the economy. Instead, it simply makes each dollar less valuable and leads to higher prices, a monetary phenomenon we call "inflation."

It is an insidious form of stealing. People feel wealthier as the numbers on their paychecks and bank balances rise. As nominal stock prices rise, people feel as though things are going well. But they don't notice the value of those dollars is eroding steadily.

Worse, it provides incentives for going into debt. People who borrowed today will repay those obligations in the future with dollars that are worth much less...

Inflation has been so prevalent for so long, most people don't even know it's not part of a normal economic system. Data on consumer prices from 1596-1971 in Britain prove that during gold-standard periods, commodity prices remain level – even over hundreds of years, during periods of massive economic growth and soaring populations.

The most important test of paper money is whether it facilitates real, per-capita economic growth. And on that score, the evidence is overwhelmingly negative.

Real wages for most Americans have been stagnant or falling for decades.

Measured in ounces of gold, per-family income in the United States has declined since 1971, retreating back to 1950s levels, despite the advent of two-income families.

Measured another way (using the government's own consumer price index as the inflation adjustment), real per-family income is essentially unchanged since 1971, again despite the fact that far more households have two wage earners today. Household earnings, in real terms, have fallen 30%-50% since the gold standard was abandoned.

The real (adjusted for inflation) median household income in the U.S. has been flat since at least 1980.

In other words, despite the boom in the economy and financial assets over the past 30 years – which boosted the fortunes and incomes of the wealthiest Americans like never before – *average* Americans are actually worse off than they were decades ago. *And they've been forced to borrow more and more simply to keep up.*

You may already be familiar with this fact...

But I bet you don't know *why* this has happened. Again, the reason is simple, but it's one most folks will never understand... and one you'll never hear an economist or government official admit.

The underlying economic cause is simply that wages are no longer connected to gains in productivity.

When money is sound and reliable, it doesn't lose value over time.

Our monetary system, however, isn't sound or reliable. Our politicians monkey with the money supply constantly. Sometimes, they increase the amount of money by huge amounts in response to demands from powerful groups, especially banks.

As a result, the things you need to live a regular life – like gasoline, milk, housing, and medical care – are constantly increasing in price. And these prices go up, year after year, even when wages don't.

That means even though our economy might grow, and even though lots of firms (like tech firms) are doing well, the average worker has gotten poorer and poorer.

If you study the data closely, you'll find that wages since the early 1970s haven't gone up at all. Sometimes they go down. Sometimes they go back up. But measured against prices, workers haven't gained an inch since the 1970s.

Here's a chart based on research from the Economic Policy Institute that describes the problem. As you can see, productivity in this country grew nearly 250% between 1948 and 2016, but median wages only grew 109%...

Productivity Growth vs. Income Growth

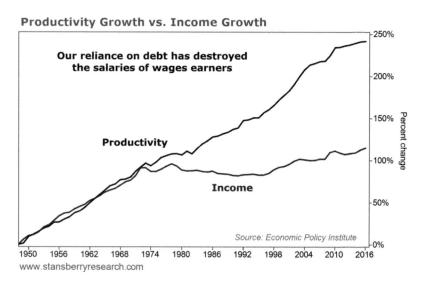

www.stansberryresearch.com

Paper money works great for the rich, who can hedge their exposure to the currency and whose access to fixed-rate credit allows huge asset purchases. But it is horrible for the middle class...

When we took the dollar off gold and allowed the central bank to continuously debase the currency, the dollar and the wages paid in the dollar no longer kept pace with inflation.

Thus, when trade or innovation leads to a gain in productivity (and the loss of a job), there is no reciprocal benefit to wages for the middle class. The replacement job is sure to come at a much lower real wage.

Any reasonable study of paper-money systems versus gold-backed monetary systems demonstrates the superiority of gold immediately. So... why does almost every modern government choose paper? The answer is because paper money allows the wealthy and powerful vested interests in our economy to manipulate interest rates, prices, the money supply, and credit to their exclusive advantage.

Think about this for a second. Imagine how much productivity in our economy has increased since 1971...

Our economy has boomed through enormous increases to productivity thanks to technologies like personal computers, cell phones, RFID tags (for inventory control), and fantastic increases to fuel efficiency.

You can see these gains in your everyday life. Lots of things have gotten better and better over the last 40 years or so.

I'd estimate productivity has increased by 4%-6% per year since 1971.

Despite our country's tremendous prosperity, the average American hasn't gotten wealthier. He's gotten poorer.

Where did all that wealth go? It didn't end up boosting the value of our currency, as you'd expect. Prices never fell. Instead, all those productivity gains were consumed by the issuance of more and more money – by inflation.

Therefore, average wages, in real terms, have declined. And all these productivity gains – all that wealth – was consumed by the financial sector, the government, debtors... all the people who benefit from inflation.

As a result, we've been left with a heavily indebted economy that's still led by consumption. Our system rewards debtors and punishes savers. It makes long-term capital investment nearly impossible because of economic volatility and financial risks caused by inflation. Worst of all, our system requires everyone become a speculator because there's no other way to safeguard savings.

What the gold standard really does is ensure a level playing field for all economic actors – borrowers, lenders, and even governments. That's why bankers (who are always highly leveraged), media barons (who constantly borrow to buy more properties), and governments (which can never balance their budgets) all abhor gold. To maintain their power, they all need paper money. The system we have now and those who profit from it would not survive a transition back to the gold standard.

The little-known reality of our paper money system is that it robs our currency of gains to purchasing power. That means the average person is working harder and producing more, but cannot buy as much as they used to. Meanwhile, asset prices have soared. The wealthy become wealthier as the value of everything they own becomes inflated along with our currency.

This explains why the wealth gap has grown so much since 2000. And it explains why the wealth gap will continue to grow, so long as our government continues its corrupt policies of quantitative easing, corporate bailouts, overspending, and over-taxing.

Simply working harder – or working smarter – isn't benefiting employees anymore. On the other hand, Americans who own assets and businesses have seen their wealth soar over the last 40 years.

It's this system that dooms every average worker to poverty and almost guarantees that the rich and the powerful will stay that way. And it is this massive gap that is ultimately fueling today's problems.

Our paper money does one other thing that I believe could ultimately bring about its own demise... It steals from our creditors.

As I've explained, borrowers today will repay their debts in devalued dollars. That's a bad deal for lenders. And at this point, America is dependent on its lenders to sustain our standard of living.

However, I believe governments and entities around the world that hold U.S. debt have grown tired of watching the value of those obligations inflated away. And I believe we're facing a mutiny on the dollar.

Part II

How to Survive
the Debt Jubilee

– Chapter 1 –

Off Limits: What You Must Avoid in the Debt Jubilee

There's no denying it...

Whether it's violent protests in major cities across the country, soaring rates of drug abuse and suicide, or even the recent national anthem controversy in the NFL, it's clear...

Something is wrong in America.

If you're like us, you can't open a newspaper or turn on the nightly news without feeling as though the fabric of civil society is being torn apart.

Most Americans believe our debt problems were "solved" during the 2008 financial crisis. You know better.

Yes, vast amounts of bad mortgage debt were wiped out. But American consumers – to say nothing of corporations or the government itself – never stopped borrowing. Our economy never really deleveraged.

In essence, we simply replaced mortgage debt with vast amounts of new consumer debt in America. We ran up our credit cards, bought fancy cars we couldn't really afford, and borrowed insane amounts of money for college degrees of questionable value.

And we now hold more total debt than ever before in history.

But it gets even worse...

Even during the peak of the housing bubble – when lenders issued lots of subprime mortgages without checking a borrower's income – most mortgages were well collateralized. Even then, most people had the income required to pay the loan.

But that is not the case today. Most of this consumer debt has been *concentrated in the poorest segments of our society.*

A huge number of Americans have borrowed more money than they can ever dream of repaying.

They have little of value to show for it. They have no way out. And they have no hope that things will get better.

What you're seeing on the news is just the tip of the iceberg...

Tens of millions of angry Americans increasingly feel they have nothing to lose.

Worst of all, this is happening despite some of the lowest interest rates in history. Debt-service costs have never been cheaper.

But interest rates are already moving higher. How many more Americans will join the ranks of their fellow indebted citizens as these massive debts become more and more costly? What happens then?

The likely 'end game' is clear...

Sooner or later, the U.S. government will have no choice but to appease these folks. They will wipe out these debts and redistribute trillions of dollars in the process. You could lose all your hard-earned savings in the turmoil.

What is coming is the largest Debt Jubilee in history. When it unfolds, trillions of dollars will be wiped out. Millions of investors, pensioners, insurance customers, and creditors will lose a fortune. Stocks will collapse. Dozens of companies will go bankrupt.

What people don't realize is that there is a ton of bad consumer debt hidden out there... in banks, credit-card companies, pension plans, auto companies, tech companies, insurance companies, homebuilders, etc. It is buried deep in the financial system.

Just one quick example...

Do you remember the "Liar Loans" from the mortgage crisis?

These were home loans in which lenders asked borrowers their income... but never bothered to verify the facts. So borrowers could make up whatever figure they wanted... and get a much more expensive house than they could afford.

Well... believe it or not, the same thing is happening again right now with auto loans.

One company – Santander Consumer USA (SC) – has made an extraordinary number of these problematic loans. A recent Bloomberg story says this firm verified the income on only 8% of the loans it made.

And guess what...

Just like the mortgage crisis of 2008, these loans have been packaged up into what are known as "asset-backed securities" (ABS) and sold to hundreds of mutual funds, insurance companies, investment firms, and even state pension plans.

Our research team found more than 120 entities that own these dangerous loan packages, just from this one company alone. I'm sure you'll recognize some of the names...

- JP Morgan Chase

- TIAA-CREF

- The State of Florida

- Blackrock

- Vanguard Group

- T Rowe Price

- Wells Fargo

- UBS

- Pacific Life Insurance Company

- Prudential Financial

- Hartford Financial Group

- Swiss RE

- Transamerica Investment Services

- London Stock Exchange Group

- Deutsche Bank

- MMM Healthcare

- Macquarie Group

- Goldman Sachs

- Invesco LTD

- Bank of New York Mellon

- Eaton Vance

- Regions Bank

- Zurich Global

- People's United Bank

- Franklin Resources

- Massachusetts Mass Mutual Insurance.

- Merrill Lynch

When the next Debt Jubilee arrives, the problems with all this bad consumer debt will hit at once. Everyone will panic.

And that's the biggest problem. The uncertainty.

No one will know for months and months how it will all get sorted out. So the markets will react violently. Right now, it's impossible to know which mechanism the government will use to implement the Jubilee...

Car companies, homebuilders, credit-card companies, insurance firms, banks, other lending institutions, and any business operating with leverage, will take a huge hit. Stocks will fall considerably. Banks will close. There will be trillions of dollars in losses.

At the end of the day, we believe the losses at an institution like Wells Fargo could be enough to start a bank run. And once a bank run starts... look out... it's nearly impossible to stop.

Now before you panic...

You should know that the mayhem that will happen around you... like higher inflation, rising interest rates, increasing debt defaults, and falling stock prices... doesn't mean it must be a crisis for you.

Here's what should you do...

Step 1:
Get Out of These Investments Now

In a credit crisis, some stocks – the most elite blue-chip capital-efficient stocks – like we mention in Part II, Chapter 2, "The Safety Fund" – will hold up better than most stocks.

But most will collapse. Bond yields are going to move much higher. That will take a huge toll on the stock market. And most stocks will fall, including the stocks in your portfolio.

If you're planning to stay with stocks of any kind, you must hedge your portfolio. You must consider buying silver, owning the world's best trophy assets, and investing in crisis-proof, inflation-proof income streams. We provide you with some ideas for these kinds of investments later in *The American Jubilee*.

And you should consider shorting stocks. Few newsletter writers recommend short positions in their publications. But it's one of the specialties of our flagship newsletter *Stansberry's Investment Advisory*.

Even if you don't want to short stocks, you should at least know which companies to avoid. The tough thing is to know where to look.

No one knows more than us about the dangers that lie waiting for unsuspecting Americans in a Debt Jubilee. We've done more work on this subject than anyone else. Our in-house team consists of equity and debt analysts, including two accountants, a financial lawyer, a former hedge-fund manager, and a global business analyst.

We've studied thousands of companies. We've looked at 40,000 corporate bond offerings. And we've compiled the ultimate list of names you do NOT want to own as America's Debt Jubilee unfolds.

The following is a list of 50 companies you should avoid. They're not official recommendations to short. These are simply 50 of the most dangerous companies in America today... They are either among the worst corporate credits in the country, have broken business models, or both.

There's a good chance you own one or more of these firms. And if you do, we suggest you stay away from them during the Debt Jubilee...

Ticker	Name	Industry	Current Mkt Cap ($B)	Debt ($B)	Debt to Asset Ratio %	Debt to EBITDA	Debt due in 3 Yrs as % of Total Debt	Free Cash Last 2 Years ($B)
TSLA	Tesla	Autos	$53.1	$7.8	30.1	24.5	29%	($4.8)
F	Ford Motor	Autos	$48.2	$146.0	59.0	11.1	19%	$19.8
GM	General Motors	Autos	$63.8	$92.7	40.4	4.2	12%	$11.6
BLDR	Builders FirstSource	Building Materials	$2.0	$1.9	60.7	5.2	1%	$0.1
SC	Santander Consumer USA	Financial Services	$5.3	$30.6	78.9	10.2	46%	($1.8)
NAVI	Navient	Financial Services	$3.2	$111.8	95.5	N/A	3%	$2.4
OMF	OneMain Holdings	Financial Services	$4.2	$14.4	77.1	8.1	17%	$2.6
ALLY	Ally Financial	Financial Services	$11.5	$55.3	33.7	10.1	32%	$1.3
WRLD	World Acceptance	Financial Services	$0.7	$0.3	36.4	2.1	100%	$0.3
PODD	Insulet	Health Care	$3.4	$0.3	74.2	106.4	20%	($0.1)
CSU	Capital Senior Living	Health Care	$0.4	$1.0	85.0	12.6	8%	$0.0
CYH	Community Health Systems	Health Care	$0.7	$14.7	70.7	63.5	27%	$0.6
BKD	Brookdale Senior Living	Health Care	$1.8	$5.2	63.3	12.1	6%	($0.1)

THC	Tenet Healthcare	Health Care	$1.4	$15.2	62.3	7.4	3%	($0.1)
AKCA	Akcea Therapeutics	Health Care	$1.1	$0.1	86.6	N/A	0%	$0.0
LKSD	LSC Communications	Industrial Goods & Services	$0.6	$0.7	40.2	2.3	12%	$0.2
CWST	Casella Waste Systems	Industrial Goods & Services	$0.8	$0.5	85.4	4.4	12%	$0.1
DE	Deere & Co	Industrial Goods & Services	$42.4	$37.5	60.1	7.8	31%	$1.3
CCO	Clear Channel Outdoor	Media	$1.4	$5.1	94.5	5.2	0%	$0.1
VIAB	Viacom	Media	$10.3	$11.2	48.3	4.3	7%	$2.9
CHK	Chesapeake Energy	Oil&Gas	$3.2	$9.9	82.7	N/A	10%	($4.3)
VTGGF	Vantage Drilling	Oil&Gas	$0.9	$0.9	80.2	N/A	16%	($0.0)
DNR	Denbury Resources	Oil&Gas	$0.4	$3.1	71.0	N/A	16%	$0.0
REN	Resolute Energy	Oil&Gas	$0.6	$0.6	85.1	11.2	0%	($0.3)
CNQ	Canadian Natural Resources	Oil&Gas	$39.4	$17.9	32.2	4.7	25%	($4.5)
WFT	Weatherford International	Oil&Gas	$3.2	$7.7	63.8	N/A	9%	($0.7)
LNG	Cheniere Energy	Oil&Gas	$10.6	$24.7	92.7	151.6	0%	($9.2)
AVP	Avon Products	Cosmetics/ Personal Care	$1.0	$1.9	54.4	4.4	13%	$0.1
HOV	Hovnanian Enterprises	Home Builders	$0.3	$1.7	95.2	18.1	32%	$0.5
TCO	Taubman Centers	REITS	$2.9	$3.4	82.5	10.1	22%	($0.3)
GGP	GGP	REITS	$17.6	$12.7	57.0	8.4	11%	$0.4
WPG	Washington Prime Group	REITS	$1.4	$3.0	65.9	7.5	10%	$0.3
SAH	Sonic Automotive	Retail	$0.9	$2.4	66.3	7.8	0%	($0.1)
RH	RH	Retail	$1.8	$1.3	70.9	6.8	27%	$0.3
CONN	Conn's	Retail	$1.0	$1.1	56.6	9.8	19%	$0.0
AN	AutoNation	Retail	$4.8	$6.5	63.7	6.4	6%	$0.5
GPI	Group 1 Automotive	Retail	$1.7	$2.7	58.1	7.0	0%	$0.1
EIGI	Endurance International	Internet	$1.2	$2.0	72.7	12.1	0%	$0.2
PBI	Pitney Bowes	Office/Business Equip	$2.6	$3.5	58.4	5.9	16%	$0.7
GOGO	Gogo	Telecom	$0.9	$0.9	69.1	10.2	0%	($0.2)
I	Intelsat	Telecom	$0.6	$14.2	111.8	8.8	22%	($0.2)
S	Sprint	Telecom	$28.2	$38.4	46.5	4.1	15%	($0.2)
GSAT	Globalstar	Telecom	$2.0	$0.6	51.2	42.0	0%	$0.0
SKYW	SkyWest	Airlines	$2.4	$2.7	49.8	22.7	0%	($0.8)

CAR	Avis Budget Group	Car Rental	$3.4	$14.9	71.7	4.2	1%	($19.6)
PNK	Pinnacle Entertainment	Entertainment	$1.4	$4.0	101.1	56.9	1%	$0.2
SGMS	Scientific Games	Entertainment	$3.9	$8.1	114.7	9.3	1%	$0.3
SEAS	SeaWorld Entertainment	Entertainment	$1.1	$1.6	72.5	6.1	3%	$0.2
RGC	Regal Entertainment	Entertainment	$2.6	$2.5	89.5	4.1	4%	$0.4
CZR	Caesars Entertainment	Lodging	$8.7	$6.8	45.9	9.8	2%	$0.0

Step 2:
Make Sure Your Bank Accounts
Are Insured by the FDIC

No one likes losing money in the markets.

In a meltdown like the global financial crisis of 2008, many people were left holding shares of financial institutions like Fannie Mae, Freddie Mac, or Lehman Brothers that went to zero. Many others like AIG, Bank of Scotland, or Merrill Lynch required rescue missions to keep them afloat. And some of America's largest banks failed.

In January 2008, Douglass National Bank in Kansas City folded and started a run of failures. Washington Mutual was the biggest financial institution to fold that year, with around $300 billion in assets.

According to the Federal Deposit Insurance Corporation (FDIC), 25 banks failed in 2008. A year later, another 140 banks failed. And in 2010, another 157 banks collapsed. Of course, many were small and private. But if you held shares at the time of their collapse, you lost every penny.

Fortunately, if you held savings at one of these failed firms... you may have had protection.

Even though these banks failed, owing billions of dollars... customers who held savings accounts protected by the FDIC did not lose their money.

Today, banks offer a wide variety of accounts to choose from including checking, savings, and certificates of deposit (CDs) among others. The

FDIC insures many of these deposits for balances up to $250,000.

FDIC insurance means that even if the bank makes disastrous loans or a bank manager absconds with the money in the vault, the FDIC will make depositors whole, up to $250,000.

We recommend you confirm with your bank manager that your bank offers FDIC insurance on your specific accounts. For more details on what the FDIC covers and what they do not, you can visit its website.

But there is one account that many Americans overlook – retirement accounts with a brokerage firm.

For many people, the money in their individual retirement account (IRA) or 401(k) represents their largest investment. This is the money saved for retirement. It's what people set aside that will pay for health care, housing, food, travel, or other interests once they stop working.

Waking up one day to find your retirement nest egg had disappeared would be devastating.

Most people know that insurance protection is important. But they often overlook what could be the largest part of the wealth.

Don't be one of them.

If the FDIC doesn't cover your investment accounts, you may still have coverage. Many investment accounts offer coverage from a non-government agency called the Securities Investor Protection Corporation (SIPC).

Please keep in mind... this doesn't protect you against bad investment advice, losses in a market crash, or a crisis. For example, investments like stocks and bonds held in your brokerage account can go up and down as the market fluctuates. The FDIC and SIPC do NOT insure losses in these holdings. However, the SIPC does protect against loss of cash and securities in customer accounts for up to $500,000 (including $250,000 in cash) if a member brokerage firm fails. You can obtain more information direct from the organization.

We urge you to contact your brokerage firm to confirm your retirement account is covered.

Now, we're going to share with you some critical information that you must understand about your bank account. This information was originally published by our friend and colleague Dr. David Eifrig Jr., editor of *Retirement Millionaire*...

Step 3:
Enroll in Your Employer's 401(k)

While nearly anyone can open a retirement account like an IRA, there are other tax-deferred accounts that may apply to you. The most popular one is the 401(k)...

It is similar to an IRA. You make contributions before taxes, and the gains add up tax-free.

The key difference with 401(k)s: You have a job, and your employer sponsors and manages the account. And if you're lucky, your employer matches contributions up to a certain limit.

If there's one financial decision that absolutely every single person needs to make, it's this... Always contribute to your 401(k) to earn the maximum employer contribution.

Skipping out on that free money is the most senseless mistake in personal finance. I cannot stress this enough: **Employer 401(k) contributions are free money... Make sure you invest enough to claim the full benefit. This is the most important financial decision there is.**

Save Taxes and Get a Pay Raise

For example, take an employer that will match half of an employee's contributions up to 6%. That means if the employee sets aside 6%, the employer adds 3% for a total of 9%. That's an instant 50% return on your money... even more when you consider the tax effect.

The most you could put into your 401(k) in 2016 was $18,000 a year. For those older than 50, they could contribute $24,000.

The potential downside of 401(k)s is that they sometimes come with limited investment options. Your employer chooses a plan manager and works out the investment options that will be included. Most plans have a decent range of funds to choose from, but it can be hard to find good, low-cost funds for every one of your asset classes.

Pick an asset allocation and find the right funds to fulfill it. The good news is that investors are getting smarter when it comes to low-cost index funds, and 401(k) administrators are offering more of them every day.

Talk to your benefits administrator and see if your company offers a self-directed 401(k). This type of account has all the benefits of a 401(k) with none of the restrictions. It works just like a regular brokerage account and allows you to buy single stocks, options, exchange-traded funds (ETFs), or mutual funds.

For those who know nothing about investing – and who don't want to learn – the restricted 401(k) probably works just fine. But if you want to take more control of your financial future, convert to a self-directed 401(k).

Step 4:
Be Careful Where You Put Your Cash

How much you can keep in cash depends on when you plan to retire and how much you've saved. The upside of cash is that it adds certainty and safety to those equations.

The downside of cash is inflation.

Inflation is the true enemy of those investing for income and living off savings. Aside from rare bouts of deflation, the value of cash consistently declines. This destroys your purchasing power.

Let's say you plan to live off your retirement for 30 years. Well, $1 in 1987 is equivalent to about $2.22 in 2017. In other words, your purchasing power has more than halved in 30 years.

Inflation averages about 2% a year. With today's low interest rates, few of the cash accounts available will outpace that.

This means that holding cash is almost certainly a losing proposition. Every dollar you hang on to is decreasing in value rather than earning a positive return in stocks or bonds.

Put another way, over a 30-year sample, cash provided a lower return than stocks 73% of the time. If you've got a long time and want to generate returns, cash is a drag on your portfolio.

However, cash is king in times of volatility... outperforming stocks 27% of the time, typically when stocks are down big. When you are most concerned with safety and liquidity, cash is exactly what you need.

The numbers are similar with bonds. Cash outperforms bonds 34% of the time.

As with every investment, when you look at where you put your cash, you need to balance yield and risk. The same goes for the cash accounts we're going to cover in this section.

Some of these cash accounts are 100% risk-free. Others claim to be low-risk, but may have hidden risks that are difficult to understand.

You need to make sure you're getting a good deal for the risks you're taking.

We'll start with the lowest-risk, most "pure" cash accounts... And we'll proceed through investments that could offer a higher yield.

No. 1: Checking and Savings Accounts

The safest cash accounts are FDIC-insured checking and savings accounts with banks.

These accounts are liquid, meaning you can access your cash almost instantly via online banking or at a branch office.

Checking accounts are a good example. You can write checks directly from your account. However, they pay little in interest. I recommend keeping your checking balance just high enough to avoid any overdrafts. Or ask your bank if it will link your checking to your savings accounts for overdraft protection.

Savings accounts offer better yield, with the same safety.

Were it not for historically low interest rates, this would be a Golden Age for savings accounts. The advent of secure online banking has removed geography from the equation. So smaller banks looking to boost deposits often offer higher rates to anyone.

Big national banks, like Bank of America and Wells Fargo, offer savings accounts that currently yield 0.01% and 0.03%, respectively. You can do much better with a little searching. Websites like Bankrate or NerdWallet can help you find the best rates.

Banks like Synchrony Bank offer accounts with yields of 1.3%, 130 times what you'd collect at Bank of America. These accounts are also FDIC-insured and have a minimum balance of $1.

Again, 1% may not seem like much to those of you who remember 3% rates on savings accounts, but that's simply not the environment we live in today. When rates rise, these high-yield savings accounts will offer heftier yields.

A word of caution: Always read the fine print to be certain that your account is FDIC-insured. Just because you've walked into an FDIC-insured institution (or visited its website), it doesn't mean every account is insured. These banks offer all kinds of products and many don't fall under the FDIC's watch.

No. 2: Money Market Accounts

One such FDIC-insured product is a money market account, or MMA.

MMAs, sometimes referred to as money market deposit accounts, will usually have higher minimum deposit requirements than a savings account, though this can be as low as $500 in some cases.

If you meet those minimums and have your checking accounts covered, MMAs almost always pay a higher rate than savings accounts, so use them when you can.

For both savings accounts and MMAs, regulations state that you can't have more than six transfers per month into or out of the accounts.

So it takes a little planning ahead to make sure that your checking balances can handle whatever you'd need.

It's important to note there is a large difference between money market *accounts* and money market *mutual funds* (MMMFs). They sound similar but have different risks. We'll cover MMMFs later on.

No. 3: Certificates of Deposit

Certificates of deposit, or CDs, have many of the benefits of savings and money market accounts. For example, they're FDIC-insured, with no risk of loss unless our entire government collapses.

They do have one drawback. But that drawback comes with a higher yield, and it just may be the perfect place to keep your cash depending on your needs.

The risk CDs carry is liquidity risk. When you put your cash in a CD, you agree to leave it there for a particular amount of time, between three months to five years.

If you want to get it back before then, you need to pay a penalty.

Since the money is locked up, the bank will give you a higher interest rate. You can collect about 1% or even 1.5% on a one-year CD from some of the more competitive banks... with higher yields for longer time periods.

Given that your money is locked up, CDs work better for the cash allocation of your portfolio as you approach retirement, not your emergency fund.

You can use what's called a "CD ladder" to match your cash needs in the future.

For instance, say you have $25,000 on hand that you want to put away as a cash allocation... You expect you'll want to cash out $5,000 a year. Each year, you can open a new five-year CD (which can yield 2.3% as of late 2017). Five years later, you'll have one CD expire each year and you can collect the cash at regular intervals. You can also reinvest it over again if you don't need it.

In the worst-case scenario, the fees associated with getting your cash early aren't too damaging. For instance, exiting a one-year Wells Fargo CD means you forfeit three months' interest and the minimum fee is $25. Check the fine print before you sign.

No. 4: Money Market Mutual Funds

All the prior cash accounts have a major advantage: They are FDIC-insured. The peace of mind that should give you can't be overstated.

When you branch out into money market mutual funds (or MMMFs), *you do not have an FDIC guarantee.* You now face the risk of loss. You have become an investor, and not a saver.

That's not how MMMFs are sold, though. They are sold as ultra-safe places to hold your cash savings. You'll see language from fund companies like "[the fund] seeks to provide current income and preserve shareholders' principal investment by maintaining a share price of $1."

This $1 share price is the central focus of MMMFs. You buy shares for $1 and the fund invests that cash in short-term securities. By law, the investments must expire within 90 days.

When the fund makes money, its share price doesn't rise. Instead, it creates more $1 shares and adds them to your account. If you check your balance, it doesn't *look* like you're an investor. It looks like your dollars are growing.

Here's the trick with MMMFs...

They are exceptionally safe... until they aren't.

MMMFs use a wide range of securities to generate their returns. There is a massive market of short-term securities that you've likely never explored.

They use securities like short-term Treasury bonds and T-bills, but they also use things like overnight repurchase agreements, or repos. This is a complex system whereby a bank will borrow $99.99 overnight and pay back $100 the next day. Of course, this is happening on the scale of trillions of dollars.

This system is called the "shadow banking" system. It works flawlessly almost all the time. But when things go wrong, there's trouble.

This is what happened in the financial crisis. In 2008, the short-term paper markets froze up. People were too scared to lend to one another, even overnight loans to the biggest banks. The market was in a panic.

A few funds got themselves into trouble. The Reserve Primary Fund was one of the largest and most respected funds, with $68 billion in assets. In particular, it had a big pile of securities issued by Lehman Brothers. Since everyone was in a panic, the fund couldn't figure out what these loans were worth.

The fund was unable to maintain its $1-per-share value. This is known as "breaking the buck."

Investors in the Reserve Fund had their cash frozen while the fund sorted things out. It was more than a year before a court ordered the fund to pay out whatever money it did have to shareholders.

Some people had hundreds of thousands of dollars in "cash"... but they couldn't access a penny.

But virtually no individual investors check the holdings of their MMMFs.

That's partly because trouble like this doesn't happen often. Prior to 2008, not a single fund broke the buck in the 37-year history of MMMFs.

So you shouldn't fear MMMFs... You just need to understand what's happening with your cash when it no longer has FDIC insurance.

There are also some tricks you can use to ensure you get the best MMMFs.

The shadow banking system is a highly efficient market. That means if a fund has a higher yield than its competitors, it's taking on more risk.

You should also check out the fees. For instance, take two funds that each yield 1% after fees. You would think that they have the same risk.

However, one might charge a 0.5% management fee while the other charges 0.25%.

That means the fund with the higher fees has to use riskier investments to get the same yield. In this case, the low-fee fund is unequivocally better than the high-fee fund.

And diversification will benefit you here as well. If you've got a substantial amount of cash and you don't want it frozen during a crisis, spread it around a few different MMMFs managed by different investment companies. Three different funds should be enough.

Here's the important thing to know today...

MMMFs do have some remote risk. And as of late 2017, their yields are not high enough to justify taking those risks relative to FDIC-insured accounts.

MMMFs, on average, yield only about 1.1%. (When you look up funds, you'll see it quoted as the seven-day yield. This uses the fund performance from the last seven days to determine its annual yield.)

That's maybe just a touch higher than you can earn in insured bank accounts or CDs. Considering you're going from zero-risk to a risky investment and getting just a few tenths of a percentage point, we consider MMMFs mostly off the table until interest rates rise.

MMMFs are going to have to yield a heck of a lot more than they do today.

You Can Make Vast Amounts of Money During the Jubilee

Every market-rattling event such as this creates both losers and big winners.

As the Jubilee unfolds, the rich and well connected are going to get richer, and the poor are going to get poorer. It's up to you to decide which side you want to be on.

In the rest of this book, we're going to walk you through several ways to survive – and even safely profit from – a crisis...

– Chapter 2 –

The Safety Fund

As we said earlier, there are 50 stocks you should stay away from during the upcoming Debt Jubilee. But that doesn't mean all stocks are on the chopping block.

If you want to keep some exposure to stocks, here is one of the most important and safest ideas for investing in them right now...

It's far more important than knowing what the economy is doing... what the government is doing... or what's happening in the news.

As the next Debt Jubilee unfolds, we want you to know about the small group of stocks you can safely hold, with as much of your investment portfolio as you want, and not have to worry about a thing.

They are among the most financially stable companies in the world, and they will not be hurt by this crisis like everything else. You can safely put your money in these companies and never look at them again for at least five years.

These companies produce extraordinary returns over the long term. One firm on our list has gained about 215% over the last five years. Another has gained 820% over the same period.

These elite businesses usually dominate their markets.

They nearly always have some competitive advantage in the market. It could be their brand, their distribution network, or a combination of several factors.

Almost without exception, these companies sell high-margin products or services in stable industries.

They generate tons of cash every year. And they regularly return more capital to shareholders than they spend on capital investments. We call these companies "capital efficient."

Most investors don't look beyond reported earnings, cash flows, and share buyback numbers to see what's really happening to the money a company earns. It should be obvious that companies that don't need ever-increasing amounts of capital to maintain their business operations – and routinely return large percentages of their profits to shareholders – should be prized far more than companies that spend every penny they earn (and more) to maintain their growth rate and keep their employees happy.

This is common sense.

If a company returns more of what it makes every year to its shareholders, then the compound return of its stock will be much, much higher over time than the returns of another company that grows its sales and profits at a similar rate but reinvests all that it earns back into its business.

There's no great wisdom in this conclusion. It's a matter of basic math. Yet this concept is beyond the scope of almost every individual investor.

Evaluating capital efficiency gives us a permanent edge in the market, because almost everyone else ignores this crucial variable... Few people even understand the concept.

What's truly important for growing wealth in stocks is the accumulation of elite, capital-efficient, dividend-paying businesses purchased at reasonable prices.

That's what using this investment strategy will do for you.

In this chapter, you'll find a list of eight companies that fit our criteria for Global Elite and capital-efficient businesses. We hope you will embrace this strategy to help build your wealth.

Let's get started...

Ralph Lauren (NYSE: RL)

Ralph Lauren (RL)

www.stansberryresearch.com

RALPH LAUREN (RL)

MARKET CAP: $7.4 BILLION

Fundamentals	2012	2013	2014	2015	2016
Revenue	$6,945	$7,450	$7,620	$7,405	$6,653
EBITDA	$1,359	$1,388	$1,329	$892	$213
Free Cash Flow	$742	$517	$503	$589	$668
Cash	$1,298	$1,285	$1,144	$1,085	$1,353
Total Assets	$5,418	$6,088	$6,106	$6,213	$5,652
Debt / Assets (%)	4.9	4.9	8.7	11.5	10.4

All dollar figures in MILLIONS unless noted.

www.stansberryresearch.com

Founded 50 years ago by its namesake, **Ralph Lauren (NYSE: RL)** is an iconic fashion brand known for its men's clothing. The clothes aren't flamboyant... They're timeless, sophisticated styles.

Businesses with elite brands, like Ralph Lauren, take decades to build. So their shares normally fetch high prices. But every now and then, they experience a temporary setback.

The important thing is that even though the share price may decline, the underlying business remains strong. The best investors always buy these stocks when they go on sale.

The rise of online-retail giant Amazon has killed many brick-and-mortar retailers. And many "big box" retailers and traditional mall anchor stores are dying a slow death. Most investors have dumped all retail stocks, even the quality ones (like Ralph Lauren). This creates an opportunity.

Though the decline of big-box retailers has hurt Ralph Lauren, what most investors are missing is that it excels in generating free cash flow (FCF). It can do this because it doesn't own or operate any production facilities. It outsources those capital-intensive tasks to hundreds of different partners.

Ralph Lauren has been called an apparel maker, but it doesn't actually make clothes. It just sells its stellar brand. This means it's highly capital efficient. As a result, Ralph Lauren has posted FCF of more than $400 million in each of the last 10 years – an impressive streak.

Ralph Lauren is also a conservatively run company. It almost always has more cash on hand than debt outstanding. In other words, there's no chance of a bankruptcy.

In July 2017, a new CEO – Patrice Louvet – took the reins. He doesn't have a fashion background, but we see that as a good thing. Louvet can focus on improving the marketing efforts and streamlining operations, while letting Ralph Lauren (the founder) carry out his creative vision as the company's chief creative officer.

Louvet spent more than 25 years at consumer-products giant Procter & Gamble and most recently ran its global beauty business. As we see it, Louvet's biggest challenge is to figure out ways to sell Ralph Lauren's brand digitally... And we believe he'll be successful.

Ralph Lauren is an authentic American brand that people will covet for many decades to come... And the cash will continue to roll in for this apparel "maker."

American Express (NYSE: AXP)

American Express (AXP)

www.stansberryresearch.com

AMERICAN EXPRESS (AXP)

MARKET CAP: $83 BILLION

Fundamentals	2012	2013	2014	2015	2016
Revenue	$33,781	$34,932	$35,895	$34,441	$33,823
EBITDA	$9,668	$10,866	$11,710	$10,604	$10,895
Free Cash Flow	$6,029	$7,541	$9,795	$9,270	$6,849
Cash	$22,250	$19,486	$22,288	$22,762	$25,208
Total Assets	$153,140	$153,375	$159,103	$161,184	$158,893
Debt / Assets (%)	40.7	39.3	38.6	32.8	33.1

All dollar figures in MILLIONS unless noted.

www.stansberryresearch.com

American Express (NYSE: AXP) began in 1850 as a horseback-delivery service. Today, it's one of the world's most recognizable financial-services firms.

There are 113 million American Express cards globally. Cardholders rack up $1 trillion-plus in charges every year. American Express offers charge cards, revolving credit cards, and travel-related services to consumers and businesses.

Marketing-research firm Interbrand estimates that the American Express brand name is the 27th-ranked brand in the world, worth nearly $18 billion. That's almost one-fourth of its $83 billion market cap.

Brands fall under what famed investor Warren Buffett – who owns more than 17% of the company in 2017 – refers to as "economic goodwill." You won't see this categorized as a line item on American Express' balance sheet or income statement. It includes things like a firm's reputation, its competitive moat, and its loyal customer base.

Don't let the accounting language baffle you. Buffett may not use the term "capital efficient" like we do. But he often talks about "economic goodwill" and "return on net tangible assets." These concepts are all measures of capital efficiency and elite businesses.

American Express is different from other credit-card companies. Because of its incredible brand and reputation, it can charge higher merchant fees – generally about 3%. Merchants will pay the higher fee because they get a wealthier type of customer. The merchant bank keeps a small, 0.25% fee. But the rest (2.75%) goes to American Express, which acts as both the processor and the card issuer.

This means American Express enjoys a valuable, triple-barreled revenue stream. It keeps the processing fee (like Visa), collects interest (like Capital One), and charges its cardholders an annual fee for the privilege of carrying one of its cards.

American Express collects nearly $3 billion per year from its customers simply for the right to carry the card.

This is a highly capital-efficient business with a ton of economic goodwill. And it looks after shareholders.

Over the past 10 years, American Express generated $325 billion in sales. Roughly $76 billion rolled into FCF. And it returned $31 billion to shareholders by way of dividends or share buybacks. In other words, for every dollar in sales, $0.23 turns into FCF. And American Express sends nearly $0.10 of every dollar in sales directly back to the shareholders.

When looking at valuing operational businesses – such as capital-efficient or Global Elite stocks – we like to compare their enterprise value (or EV, which is market cap plus net debt) with their cash earnings – or earnings before interest, taxes, depreciation, and amortization (EBITDA).

EV tells us what the business would be worth if it were taken private and you bought it outright. And EBITDA tells us how the business is doing before any financial or accounting transactions come into play.

When we first recommended AXP to our subscribers in August 2016, it traded for seven times EBITDA. Over the last 10 years, AXP's EV has traded on average for about 10 times EBITDA.

Facebook (Nasdaq: FB)

Facebook (FB)

www.stansberryresearch.com

FACEBOOK (FB)

MARKET CAP: $510 BILLION

Fundamentals	2012	2013	2014	2015	2016
Revenue	$5,089	$7,872	$12,466	$17,928	$27,638
EBITDA	$1,187	$3,815	$6,237	$8,170	$14,769
Free Cash Flow	$377	$2,860	$5,495	$7,797	$11,617
Cash	$9,626	$11,449	$11,199	$18,434	$29,449
Total Assets	$15,103	$17,895	$39,966	$49,407	$64,961
Debt / Assets (%)	15.6	2.7	0.6	0.2	0.0

All dollar figures in MILLIONS unless noted.

www.stansberryresearch.com

Facebook (Nasdaq: FB) is the world's most valuable social network.

The company's website offers a platform to share information (pictures, video, and opinions). Facebook now boasts more than 2 billion users.

Harvard student Mark Zuckerberg began Facebook in 2004 as an online version of the university's student directory. Eight years later, the company began publicly trading. It remains in the top five largest initial public offerings (IPOs) in U.S. history.

Users take photos, go shopping, and travel... And they share it all on Facebook. It is a living, breathing book. And it's all about you... the user. That's what makes Facebook's users extremely valuable.

Facebook can tailor advertisements around what it knows about its users. That's how it monetizes the so-called "network effect" – that is, it grows in value the more people use it. The more users... the more valuable their data is to advertisers.

Already, the company's focused advertising generates billions of dollars in revenue. And it's growing at an incredible rate – more than 360% from 2013 to 2017. We expect that revenue growth to continue... especially as more and more financial transactions find their way onto Facebook's network.

It's also an incredibly profitable, scalable business on its own. In 2016, roughly 52% of sales turned into cash profits. Even after pouring $3 billion into capital expenditures (capex), it generated $6 billion in FCF – 34% of sales. Its scale, growth, and profitability put it into a class nearly by itself.

Facebook has also positioned itself to break into new revenue streams from messenger services like WhatsApp and Instagram, and it's prepared for new technologies like 4K screens, phones with 3D cameras, and virtual reality.

It is already one of the most capital-efficient, fastest-growing businesses the world has ever seen. And incredibly, as it grows even bigger, it will become even more capital efficient.

Facebook is a growth-stock story. Traditional valuation metrics don't make much sense to us for these companies because you are buying the earnings potential.

NVR (NYSE: NVR)

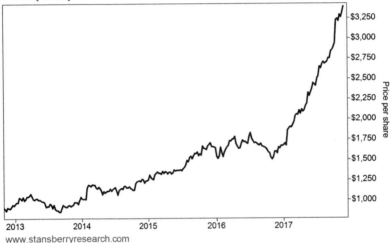

NVR (NVR)

www.stansberryresearch.com

NVR (NVR)

MARKET CAP: $12 BILLION

Fundamentals	2012	2013	2014	2015	2016
Revenue	$3,185	$4,211	$4,445	$5,159	$5,823
EBITDA	$290	$454	$494	$641	$697
Free Cash Flow	$252	$251	$153	$185	$362
Cash	$1,153	$866	$545	$424	$395
Total Assets	$2,605	$2,486	$2,351	$2,512	$2,644
Debt / Assets (%)	23.0	24.1	25.5	23.7	22.6

All dollar figures in MILLIONS unless noted.

www.stansberryresearch.com

If you're a homeowner, you'll be happy to hear that the U.S. real estate market has fully recovered from its bust since 2011...

New home sales are running at an annual rate of around 667,000, which is the highest it's been in nearly 10 years. The average nationwide home price has rebounded back above mid-2006 levels.

And even though interest rates have risen since mid-2016, the benchmark 30-year fixed mortgage rate is still less than 4% in late 2017, which is low by historical standards.

These macro trends are favorable for homebuilders. And we consider **NVR (NYSE: NVR)** to be the best homebuilder by a wide margin.

Founded in 1980 as NVHomes, NVR builds single-family detached homes, town houses, and condominium buildings. The mid-Atlantic region accounts for more than half of NVR's revenues. Washington, D.C., Baltimore, and Philadelphia are its three largest markets.

There's a reason why NVR is capital efficient... In the late 1980s and early 1990s, a real estate downturn crushed the value of NVR's land investments and forced the company into bankruptcy. The experience led the company to adopt a "land light" business model after it reorganized.

NVR now owns very little land. Instead, it purchases options from land developers, paying them a small deposit upfront to hold the lots. It pays the rest only when it's ready to start building homes. As a result, NVR carries a smaller lot inventory than other builders.

This capital-efficient strategy enabled NVR to maintain profitability every year during the 2007-2011 housing bust. And over the past five years, NVR's return on assets (ROA) has been more than 10% on average – the highest average ROA of any U.S. homebuilder. NVR's high returns have allowed for sizeable stock buybacks. NVR's shares outstanding decreased by 24% from 2011 to 2017.

Over the past 10 years, NVR's EV has traded on average for about 10 times EBITDA.

Tencent Holdings (OTC: TCEHY)

Tencent Holdings (TCEHY)

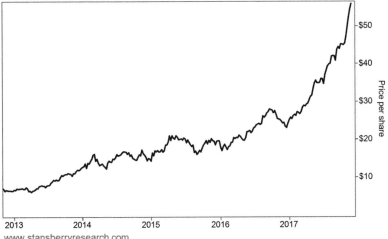

TENCENT HOLDINGS (TCEHY)

MARKET CAP: $425 BILLION

Fundamentals	2012	2013	2014	2015	2016
Revenue	$6,957	$9,831	$12,811	$16,371	$22,880
EBITDA	$2,672	$3,412	$5,444	$7,114	$9,890
Free Cash Flow	$2,619	$3,348	$4,894	$6,324	$8,742
Cash	$4,361	$6,584	$8,621	$12,635	$17,850
Total Assets	$12,070	$17,718	$27,575	$47,294	$57,048
Debt / Assets (%)	14.2	14.0	21.1	21.3	27.7

All dollar figures in MILLIONS unless noted.

Tencent (OTC: TCEHY) – the Chinese mobile chat and gaming technology firm – is the seventh-largest company in the world... And it's still growing rapidly. Its core businesses are social networks, advertising, and gaming.

The battle in China is for people's screen time... And Tencent controls screen time even better than Facebook or anything else in America.

The company's two main social networks are QQ and WeChat. QQ has more than 650 million active users, while WeChat boasts an incredible 963 million. According to Tencent, the two networks exist for different audiences.

It's a bit like the Snapchat and Facebook markets in the United States... QQ is closer to Snapchat, which connects to a younger, more entertainment-focused user. WeChat is closer to Facebook, which draws an older user base.

Even more exciting are the mobile-payment possibilities in these social networks. Both WeChat and QQ allow users to link their bank accounts and make secure payments directly from their phones. Today, WeChat and QQ have more than 300 million bank accounts linked to their mobile payment system, making it the second-largest mobile payment system in China.

That's part of what makes Tencent "sticky," as the tech gurus say. Users can't stop using its products.

Whether you're hailing a taxi, paying your bills, chatting with friends, or playing games online, you never have to leave Tencent's world.

Tencent is also the leader in mobile gaming in China. Tencent fully owns Riot Games, the creator of the popular online game *League of Legends*. And it has partnered with companies like Electronic Arts and Activision Blizzard to bring online versions of *FIFA Soccer*, *NBA 2K*, and *Call of Duty*, among others, to China.

Not only is Tencent China's mobile-gaming leader, but it's also the world's largest based on gaming revenues. It's ahead of Apple, Microsoft, Sony, and the rest. And its market share is increasing fast.

Since Tencent controls the screen time of Chinese citizens better than anyone, it's perfectly positioned for selling ads. These ad sales come from within Tencent's social networks as well as from its news and video services (think Google News and YouTube).

Tencent has done an incredible job of growing and profiting from these three lines of business – social networks, electronic gaming, and online advertising.

Tencent's sales have grown from about $350 million in 2006 to nearly $23 billion in 2016. And analysts expect Tencent to more than double its revenue from 2016 to 2018. That crazy growth is more like what you see in a startup than a company already worth more than $400 billion.

To say the future is bright would be an understatement. Tencent is doing everything right. It's growing at startup pace. And that's why we believe it can become the world's most valuable business at some point in the next five years.

Like Facebook, Tencent is a growth story, so we don't consider traditional valuation metrics.

Hershey (NYSE: HSY)

Hershey (HSY)

www.stansberryresearch.com

HERSHEY (HSY)

MARKET CAP: $22 BILLION

Fundamentals	2012	2013	2014	2015	2016
Revenue	$6,644	$7,146	$7,422	$7,387	$7,440
EBITDA	$1,321	$1,541	$1,604	$1,283	$1,508
Free Cash Flow	$836	$865	$498	$858	$714
Cash	$728	$1,119	$472	$347	$297
Total Assets	$4,755	$5,357	$5,623	$5,344	$5,524
Debt / Assets (%)	40.1	36.6	38.7	45.3	53.9

All dollar figures in MILLIONS unless noted.

www.stansberryresearch.com

Hershey (NYSE: HSY) is the largest chocolate and confection maker in the U.S... And it has one of the most cherished and revered brand names in the world.

The Hershey Trust Company has control over Hershey via its 100% ownership of Hershey's class B shares. Milton Hershey – the founder of Hershey – established this trust in 1905 to benefit the Milton Hershey School.

Hershey is so loved that the state of Pennsylvania intervened when the trust moved to sell its stake in 2002 to diversify its base of assets. The government actually made it against the law for the trust to sell the business or to buy another business that would dilute its stake in Hershey.

We're fine with the trust running things because we literally have a government guarantee that the board of directors won't do anything stupid.

Hershey is the quintessential capital-efficient company, too.

Despite operating in a slow-growth industry, Hershey grew its revenues from $5 billion in 2007 to an estimated $7.5 billion in 2017. That's a 50% increase in a decade.

But it hasn't had to grow its capex as fast to fuel its growth. Hershey's annual capex is still less than $300 million in 2017. That's less than 4% of revenues.

Without having to plow much money back into the business, Hershey's management can be extremely friendly to shareholders...

The company distributes a large portion of profits as dividends, which it has paid for more than 351 consecutive quarters (nearly 90 years).

Over the past decade, the company's annual dividends have averaged about 23% of net income. And its total annual dividend has eclipsed $500 million for the first time thanks to nine dividend hikes since 2010.

On top of that, Hershey consistently repurchases its shares. In 2016 alone, it reduced its shares outstanding (class A shares) by 2.9%.

On a combined basis (dividends and buybacks), the company has effectively paid out every single penny it has made over the past 10 years.

We recommended HSY in December 2007 with the stock trading for around $40 per share. Its EV traded for about 10 times EBITDA back then – an absolute bargain. Its 10-year average is around 13 times EBITDA.

Microsoft (Nasdaq: MSFT)

Microsoft (MSFT)

www.stansberryresearch.com

MICROSOFT (MSFT)

MARKET CAP: $655 BILLION

Fundamentals	2012	2013	2014	2015	2016
Revenue	$73,723	$77,849	$86,833	$93,580	$85,320
EBITDA	$24,730	$30,519	$32,971	$24,118	$26,804
Free Cash Flow	$29,321	$24,576	$26,746	$23,724	$24,982
Cash	$63,040	$77,022	$85,709	$96,526	$113,240
Total Assets	$121,271	$142,431	$172,384	$174,472	$193,468
Debt / Assets (%)	9.8	11.0	13.1	20.2	27.6

All dollar figures in MILLIONS unless noted.

www.stansberryresearch.com

Computer software may be the easiest business to scale.

Just think... Once the computer code is written, it doesn't cost much to copy and distribute it to another person, or millions of people. You don't have to build more factories, acquire loads of raw materials, or hire more workers.

Indeed, computer software is an inherently capital-efficient industry. And **Microsoft (Nasdaq: MSFT)** is the world's largest software maker.

After dropping out of Harvard at age 19, Bill Gates co-founded Microsoft with his childhood friend Paul Allen in 1975. Microsoft's rise began when IBM asked it to create an operating system for IBM's computers in 1980.

Microsoft went on to develop the Windows operating system and Office application suite – both of which now dominate their respective markets. Today, Windows controls more than 80% of the personal computer operating system market. Windows 10 is on more than 500 million devices around the world. And more than 120 million people use Office 365.

Microsoft also sells to businesses... It has a wide range of server products, tools, and enterprise software solutions.

Microsoft's various businesses produce enormous amounts of operating cash flow. And like we said, the capital-efficient nature of software means Microsoft doesn't have huge capex needs. Therefore, few companies generate as much FCF (operating cash flow minus capex) as Microsoft.

Microsoft's annual FCF now exceeds $30 billion per year. And its FCF as a percentage of revenue has averaged 30% over the past five years. In other words, for every dollar of revenue, Microsoft produces $0.30 of FCF. Most companies are lucky if their FCF is more than 10% of revenues... Microsoft's is three times that.

With that much FCF, Microsoft's management can return massive amounts of capital to shareholders. Last year, Microsoft paid out nearly $12 billion in dividends. And it bought back another $11 billion in stock.

Returned capital (including dividends and buybacks) has totaled $100 billion over the past five years. This goes to show just how rewarding to shareholders a capital-efficient business can be.

We recommended Microsoft in February 2012 with shares trading at $30 and an EV/EBITDA of a little more than seven – an incredible bargain. Its 10-year average EV/EBITDA ratio is 10 – a valuation we consider an excellent value for this Global Elite business.

Corning (NYSE: GLW)

Corning (GLW)

www.stansberryresearch.com

CORNING (GLW)

MARKET CAP: $28 BILLION

Fundamentals	2012	2013	2014	2015	2016
Revenue	$8,012	$7,819	$9,715	$9,111	$9,390
EBITDA	$2,176	$2,373	$3,131	$2,506	$2,586
Free Cash Flow	$1,405	$1,768	$3,633	$1,559	$1,391
Cash	$6,144	$5,235	$6,068	$4,600	$5,291
Total Assets	$29,375	$28,478	$30,063	$28,527	$27,899
Debt / Assets (%)	11.8	11.6	10.9	15.6	14.0

All dollar figures in MILLIONS unless noted.

www.stansberryresearch.com

Corning (NYSE: GLW) is *the* leader in glass technology.

The company has pioneered techniques to mass-produce everything from light bulb encasements to television picture tubes.

You may even have some of Corning's thin yet shatter-resistant glass – called Gorilla Glass – in your pocket right now. In 2007, Corning started mass producing Gorilla Glass for Apple's first iPhone.

Gorilla Glass is now in its fifth generation, and it has become a standard for smartphones and tablet screens. Cumulatively, more than 5 billion devices around the world contain Gorilla Glass. In addition to Apple, big name brands like Samsung, LG Electronics, Toshiba, and HTC all use it. And the glass is now even being used for household and automotive applications.

Corning is also a glass-substrate producer for liquid-crystal displays (LCDs). These go into televisions, computer screens, laptops, and numerous other display screens.

Additionally, Corning sells fiber-optic cable. The new mobile wireless standard – 5G – is coming. And that means North American telecom companies need to upgrade their fiber-optic networks to support more data and keep up with consumer demand. Global optical-fiber demand is already set to increase by more than 45 million kilometers to 325 million kilometers between 2015 and 2018. Corning invented fiber-optic cable and remains a dominant player in the industry.

Increasingly, fiber is connecting more than the nodes on a global network. Traditionally, fiber connections run to the building – and from there, copper coaxial cable runs to your computer. But getting fiber to your desk eliminates additional connections and bridges, making it faster and more robust.

One key enabling technology for fiber within buildings is Corning's ClearCurve optical fiber. Historically, fiber could not be bent without losing the signal. ClearCurve fixes that problem. You can wrap it around your finger 10 times with minimal signal loss. That bendable fiber is perfect within buildings or homes, to bend around walls and ceilings, and to run right into your computer.

To maintain its edge in these advanced markets, Corning plows a significant amount of cash back into research and development (R&D). The company has spent more than $700 million on R&D in each of the last five years.

However, Corning's businesses generate so much cash flow that management can still return large amounts of capital to shareholders...

Corning generated $44 billion in sales from 2012 to 2016. It sent $14 billion – roughly 32% of sales – back to shareholders by way of dividends and share buybacks. What we really like is that Corning has bought back shares when they were selling cheap. Often, management does the opposite. But here, Corning has excelled.

Corning estimates that it will generate more than $26 billion of cash through 2019. Of that, the company plans to invest around $10 billion back into the business. This includes capex, R&D, and potential acquisitions.

Even after its capex and R&D expenses, the company still expects to send more than $12.5 billion in FCF back to shareholders. It'll do this through dividends and share buybacks.

Corning has been a leader in glass and materials development for more than a hundred years. We expect it to continue to innovate... and reward shareholders accordingly.

– Chapter 3 –

The Nine Most Important Things I'm Doing to Prepare for a Crisis in America

Porter note: In May 2014, I sat down for a lengthy interview about what steps I'd take personally to prepare for a financial crisis in America.

In the edited transcript that follows, you'll learn what I consider the nine most important steps for protecting your money, your assets, your safety, and your family.

———————————●———————————

Stansberry Research: Porter, you have been predicting a major crisis here in America for a few years now. I suspect most of our readers know that doesn't mean you think the world will end. But many of them may not be entirely sure about what you think is going to happen.

Porter Stansberry: First, I want to clarify that a major crisis is already going on in our country – and around the world, for that matter. Most people don't realize it. But a currency crisis has been ongoing in the U.S. dollar for years. All you need to do is look at the facts...

The U.S. dollar has lost roughly half of its purchasing power in the last 15 years. You need to spend twice as much cash to purchase something as you had to pay in 1999 or 2000 for the same item.

That's really not long ago. So this is a continual currency crisis that we're living in now. The real question people should be asking is whether it's likely to accelerate.

Stansberry Research: Is that where the signs are pointing?

Porter: It's common knowledge that the U.S. economy has an unsustainable debt load. And it's only getting worse. The easiest way for the government to get out of that debt is for the central bank to print a lot of money.

And that's what they're doing... How do we know? Because they're not hiding any of it. So it's only a matter of time until there's a significant loss of purchasing power. When everyday items get expensive, people are going to notice and become upset.

Stansberry Research: That sounds gloomy...

Porter: I'm not saying we'll experience a complete societal collapse. There are several different ways this could unfold. But one thing is for sure: We will have a major currency crisis on our hands soon. It could last a few days, a week, or much longer. But regardless... I'm not worried, personally. I'm confident in the steps I've taken to protect myself and my family.

While I don't ever want something like this to happen – it's going to hurt a lot of hard-working U.S. folks – I'm not going to let denial catch me unprepared. In a situation like this, some things you want to do are just logical.

For example, economies essentially shut down for relatively long periods of time during a currency crisis.

During the 2001-2002 crisis in Argentina, no banking was available at all for a period of about six weeks. There were no ATMs. There was no ability to write checks. There was nothing. The whole economy ground to a halt.

It became basically a barter system. There wasn't enough cash to drive all the transactions. If you didn't have the world's reserve currency – U.S. dollars – you couldn't buy anything. You had to trade for it.

I remember my business partners, whom I probably shouldn't mention by name, bought either a townhouse or an apartment, I forget. But they bought some real estate down there in the middle of that crisis. An attorney had to fly to Argentina to close the deal at a bank. The Argentine seller wanted $300,000 for a property that was worth more than $1 million... But he would only do the deal in U.S. dollars and in cash.

So they wired $300,000 down there, and the attorney pushed it across the table to the seller. The Argentine counted one stack of 100 bills, counted all the stacks, and passed the keys over to their attorney. And the deal was done. The Argentine put the cash in a briefcase and walked out the door. It was classic.

Most Americans have no concept that this type of situation could happen here. People forget that banks have very little cash on hand. The reserve ratio of the U.S. banking industry has been on a steady decline since World War II. So we're more and more at risk of a major bank run.

And let's be honest – being prepared for something like this just makes good common sense. How do you know that there won't be some computer virus that shuts down the power grid or causes banks to have errors? If 11 transformers blew up, the whole national power grid would fail. This wouldn't necessarily have to be the result of terrorism. It could just be a mistake.

A situation like this may not last long. They would probably be able to fix that in a couple days. But we could always face a situation where for a period of three to five days, you don't have access to any kind of banking. So the first thing that I would urge people to do is to have **a safe place outside the bank to store a reasonable amount of currency, gold, and silver**... and believe it or not, also guns and ammunition.

Stansberry Research: When you talk about holding cash, are you referring to the U.S. dollar?

Porter: Yes, because the U.S. dollar still remains the world's reserve currency. Now if you really wanted to protect yourself, you could diversify easily. You could get some euros. I would maybe get some Canadian dollars. That seems to be a much safer alternative because it's a commodity-based currency.

The safe currencies are basically going to be the Swiss franc, the Singapore dollar, and the Canadian dollar. I imagine you would be safe with a healthy mix of any of those currencies.

Stansberry Research: Where exactly do you suggest storing it? In your house or a safety deposit box?

Porter: Well, I'm not going to tell you exactly where I keep my money...

That wouldn't make it very safe, now would it?

All kidding aside, it's reasonably secure to keep these things in a safe somewhere in your house or on some piece of property you own. But make sure the safe is well-hidden. I wouldn't leave it in my closet.

And you don't have to spend a fortune on this kind of thing. A simple way to do this is to get a self-storage unit. They have 24-hour surveillance. And you use your own lock. Who's going to go looking in a self-storage unit for gold bullion? It's not going to happen. So you could just put a small safe in a self-storage unit and put a bunch of other junk on top of it.

So if somebody does happen to break into it, what are they going to see? Just junk. They're not going to find your bullion. Just make sure that you don't tell anyone where you've hidden your gold, and you pay your storage fees.

Another obviously cheap solution is burying it. You can rent a Bobcat for a day and bury anything you want. If you do that, be careful you don't run into power lines or sewer lines.

Some of this may sound a bit crazy, but it's crazier to be unprepared. The far more dangerous thing is not taking these precautions, right? You're not increasing your risk by taking a small amount of currency and bullion and pulling it out of the bank. You're actually reducing your risk.

Stansberry Research: It certainly can't hurt.

Porter: But really the gold standard is a Swiss passport. If you have all the money in the world and you want the ultimate bug-out plan, then get an apartment in Zurich and a Swiss passport. You can get that done for about $5 million.

Stansberry Research: Well that's great, but how many people can actually afford to do that?

Porter: Not many. Like I said, it's the gold standard. That's what I'm working for. But the important thing I want to get across is that you need to become less U.S.-dependent.

I'll give you another kind of extreme example. I have a friend who is the UN council of some tiny island nation in the Pacific. Someplace I can't pronounce.

He gave the government there a quarter-million dollars or so, and they made him part of their UN staff. So he has a diplomatic passport that allows him to travel anywhere in the world.

Stansberry Research: So what could someone who isn't a millionaire do to become less U.S.-dependent?

Porter: It depends on where you live. I have a large fishing yacht in Miami. If I lived there full-time, I would get a bank account in the Bahamas with a safety deposit box. That would be a very easy solution for me. It's easy for me to transfer bullion and paper bills to those locations. If you live in the northeast, Canada is a great solution. Or if you live near the U.S/ Mexico border, then you can do the same in Mexico.

The idea is just to diversify your savings in a way that would allow you to prosper even in the event of a breakdown of the U.S. banking system, whether that was due to a currency collapse or due to a technological failure or due to some kind of malfeasance. You know, maybe hackers break into your bank and steal all the money or something.

Stansberry Research: So just to reiterate, you think the most important things our readers can do in preparation for a currency crisis are having some of their assets outside a bank and becoming less U.S.-dependent...

Porter: Yes, but don't forget about having plenty of currency on hand. And that is especially true if you are traveling.

I've got a good story about that, by the way...

What would you say is generally associated with carrying large sums of cash? After all, it is very frowned upon in the world.

Stansberry Research: I don't know... Probably drugs or prostitution. Something illicit like that.

Porter: Right, it is very frowned upon in the world. But a lot of the older, very successful people I know simply think it's prudent to carry a large amount of cash. So one senior newsletter writer I know very well always carries at least $100,000 in cash with him everywhere he goes, and it came in handy one time we were traveling in Argentina...

We were in the Salta Province in northwest Argentina, and it was about 7 o'clock at night. Once we got to where we were going, a close colleague of mine picked up a call on his cell phone from his wife. She said the worst thing you could possibly imagine hearing, "Our daughter has viral meningitis, and she's not going to live through the night. You have to come as soon as you can."

So think about that...

It's 7 o'clock at night. You're in the middle of nowhere in rural Argentina. And your daughter's not going to live until the morning, what do you do?

What would any good friend do? You pick up the phone and call the concierge at the hotel back in Buenos Aires. You say, "My colleague's daughter is dying back in the U.S. We need a Gulfstream here ASAP, and we need to get my friend to the hospital back in the U.S. as quickly as is humanly possible."

And the concierge says, "The plane will leave in 45 minutes." He hangs up and makes it happen.

The plane is in the air. The pilot calls me. "Listen, buddy, we're in the air, but I'm turning the plane around right now unless you can assure me that there's $85,000 in cash when we land."

"How about we wire it to your bank in the morning?" I ask. "No can do," he says. "We need it on the tarmac."

There are 10 of us in the group. Now, it's 9 o'clock at night, and of course, we're still in the middle of nowhere, Argentina. "Hey, anybody got $85,000 I can borrow?" I ask.

That's not a made-up story. That really happened. I was there, and there was no substitute for having $100,000 in cash. My cash-carrying friend saved the day. Without this cash on hand, there's no way this could have happened.

Stansberry Research: Was his daughter OK?

Porter: It's a long story, but eventually he got there at around 2 p.m. the next day. And fortunately, his daughter survived.

Stansberry Research: Wow.

Porter: But yeah, it was unpleasant. Anyway, things can happen... especially if you're traveling. Often when those things happen, there is no substitute for cash. A lot of times when I'm on my boat in the Bahamas and we're running low on fuel, we'll find an island with a tiny dock... like you'd see on a Microsoft screensaver, you know?

There's a little tiny island with one dock and a Texaco fuel pump. You know there's no way you can use a credit card because the cellular system's never working. So unless you have cash, it's a no-go.

Stansberry Research: Those are some amazing stories. It really sounds like something straight out of a movie, but I'm glad his daughter was OK.

Porter: Trust me, it's not something you want to go through. My son got very sick and was hospitalized for a while. It puts things in perspective. Nothing's more important than your family's health.

But people don't think about that sort of thing. If something were to happen – even if you couldn't go to a pharmacy for a few days – do you think people are prepared for that?

No way, nobody even considers what it would be like if you couldn't get medicine or go to the grocery store for a week or a month at a time. If you require medication for your health...

Stansberry Research: Or your kids...

Porter: Right, especially if you're a diabetic or something like that. Believe me, those things will be the most important things to have stockpiled.

Stansberry Research: Even basic antibiotics.

Porter: Yes, it's smart to have a secret stash of antibiotics and first-aid supplies. I don't want you to think I'm a "doomsday prepper"... I'm not.

I don't think it makes any sense to believe you can live in a hole in the ground for a year. But I definitely believe in having the resources and the ability to take care of yourself and your family for a seven- to 10-day emergency period... and ideally having the wherewithal to be able to leave the country if the crisis were to get worse.

Stansberry Research: It's always smart to have an exit strategy...

Porter: Definitely. I would have an escape plan, not a hole in the ground. But in any case, it's reasonable to keep a seven- to 10-day supply of cash, medicines, food, water, and guns and ammunition. There's no doubt that the social order in our country could break down.

Stansberry Research: But if the social order seriously begins to break down during a currency crisis and things get dangerous, what can our readers to do, other than trying to get out of the United States? I mean, that might not be an option for everybody.

Porter: Right, it probably isn't. I can tell you which neighborhoods you don't want to go into. And I think we all know where those places are.

Stansberry Research: Don't head to Baltimore?

Porter: Don't head to Baltimore.

I saw a recent infographic yesterday in Chicago that showed the demographics of the city. It showed how the very poor had expanded out into the suburbs in Chicago, and the very rich had become more and more isolated in the center of the city on the shore.

I would try to find a way to get to any of the 50 or so places in the country that have real concentrations of wealth. You know those signs that say, "We accept EBT"?

Stansberry Research: Yeah, those are places that take food stamps, right?

Porter: Exactly. Those are the areas you want to avoid.

Stansberry Research: I get what you're saying. But couldn't the really wealthy areas become a target? If you're in the center of the city with all the wealth but surrounded on all sides by neighborhoods where people are collecting food stamps, is that really a good idea?

Porter: Yeah, in fact it is. That's where I want to be. The rich people are going to take care of themselves. I remember when Hurricane Katrina hit New Orleans. The people living in one really wealthy neighborhood, Audubon Place, flew in a team of Israeli mercenaries on a private jet and put their whole neighborhood on lock down. Nobody came in or out.

Stansberry Research: Not a bad private security force to have in a pinch.

Porter: Exactly. So if you asked me whether I'd rather be in Compton or Beverly Hills, I'm going take Beverly Hills. And this type of advice applies to everyone. If you have the option to live in a big house in a transitioning neighborhood or an apartment in a wealthy area, it's safer to choose the apartment every time.

Stansberry Research: I was just suggesting that maybe you would leave the city and go out into a more rural area?

Porter: If you study past breakdowns of society – the riots in '68, for example, here in Baltimore or the ones in Detroit – the rioters always burn their own stores.

And just think about it. People out in Baltimore County are armed to the teeth. You don't want to go there.

Stansberry Research: Yeah, you probably don't want to test your mettle against a bunch of angry farmer's with shotguns. Since we are on the subject, any other worst-case-scenario precautions? What about generators or anything like that? I know you're not a prepper, but being without power for a week or a month during a crisis seems like it could make things worse.

Porter: Listen, if you can afford it, a generator is always a smart idea. Plus, they are great for things like hurricanes, blizzards, or even just Baltimore's power grid. I've got backup generators and all that, but...

Stansberry Research: Do they run on natural gas?

Porter: They run on propane. I've got really big propane tanks. But they're only going to keep that generator going for a maximum of seven to 10 days before it runs out of fuel. So I don't really think that generators are the answer except for in a very short-term scenario, like a hurricane or a power outage.

Like I said, if there's a crisis that's going to be longer than a week, I'm not staying... I'm leaving.

Stansberry Research: Got it.

Porter: And so I think the best thing you could have is a boat or the ability to get to Canada or to Mexico or somewhere of your choice. But I don't think of this as a currency crisis precaution... more like an end-of-the-world thing. Most of the precautions people should take are really just common-sense kind of things.

Stansberry Research: Like what?

Porter: I'd recommend like once a year maybe go through a folder in your safe that has your critical documents: birth certificates (the originals), your passport, your insurance policies, etc. All those critical documents should be in the same place. I do it on my birthday.

I also have a cover letter on my folder that tells my wife where all of our assets are, what the account numbers and passwords are. All that stuff.

And you might say that's a security vulnerability. It is. But if they've already broken in and forced me to open my bullion safe, I got bigger problems than the fact that they now have all my account numbers and passwords.

Stansberry Research: What about specific cash holdings? I know you said to have cash on hand, but people always wonder exactly how much cash they actually need. How much should I have in cash?

Porter: A good thing is to have enough cash so that you can pay all your bills for 30 days. Figure out what your requirement of cash is for 30 days and assume that you can't write a check or go to the ATM machine. I don't think you have to be paranoid to know you don't want to end up in a situation where you don't have any money.

Stansberry Research: And gold or silver? How much gold should people keep on hand?

Porter: I think it makes sense to hold, you know, 5% to 10% of your net worth in precious metals. And whether it's gold or silver really doesn't make any difference. I would look at the silver-to-gold ratio, and I would allocate the value.

Traditionally, the "gold to silver" ratio has been as low as 16 to 1. Meaning the price of an ounce of gold cost 16 times more than the price of an ounce of silver.

In recent years, the ratio has been much higher than 16 to 1. If it's above 50, I would probably buy silver. Meaning if gold is 50 times more expensive than silver, then I think silver's cheap relative to gold. If the silver ratio is 25, then I would buy gold.

And what I do is very simple. Every year in January, when I'm done paying my taxes and paying off my Christmas gifts, I take the money left over from the previous year, call up my broker, and put it into gold bullion. I've never sold a single ounce of it. And to tell you the honest-to-God truth, I don't even know exactly how much I own. I just keep putting it in a pile, so to speak.

I just don't keep all that much money in my checking account. Anyone who reads my newsletter knows I don't recommend keeping much money in your checking account. I keep far more of my assets in my brokerage account.

Stansberry Research: Do you have the physical, paper shares?

Porter: No, I don't bother with any of that.

Stansberry Research: You're not worried that all of that just might disappear one day?

Porter: I'm not worried about it.

Stansberry Research: All that money in your brokerage account?

Porter: I have a significant portion of my net worth in physical things – houses, farms, gold, and real estate. I've got a business that's worth a lot. So if the worst were to come, I'm sure I'd be OK. Henry Ford has a great quote that your only real security in life is the people that you know and the skills that you have. So I don't live in fear.

But for people who are retired, these are much more important questions. Those folks want to make sure that they understand who controls the title to things. And if they're going to own stocks like Hershey forever, it might make a lot of sense to demand the paper shares and put them in the vault. It can't hurt.

Stansberry Research: If you don't plan on selling them any time soon...

Porter: Yes, and in fact, that might be a really useful thing for some people. A lot of people have a really hard time just sitting still and hanging on to financial assets because you can just go trade them any time you want. So if you find yourself having that problem of not being able to hold onto things for the long term, then get the paper stock.

Stansberry Research: I've been thinking about doing that myself lately. I have some stock that I don't plan on selling for at least a decade or two.

Porter: That's smart then. It can also be very comforting.

Stansberry Research: Yes... until you start worrying if there's a fire.

Porter: Well, I'm sure there's a corporate registry if that were to happen. I believe there's an account somewhere that shows that you own a certain percentage of the shares.

*[**Editor's note:** It is possible to recover your stock if your physical shares are lost, stolen, or otherwise damaged. Typically, you must contact the company's transfer agent, and it will help you begin the process of recovering your shares. You will have to give the details surrounding the loss of the shares, as well as provide some information to verify that you are indeed the rightful owner.]*

Stansberry Research: Speaking of stocks, Porter, what kind of investments should people make to protect themselves and some of their money during a currency crisis?

Porter: The important thing you want to do is make sure that your savings are being held in an asset that can manage an environment of sharply rising prices. So the most important thing for you to do is to not own bonds, especially low-quality, long-term bonds trading at or above par. There is a mania in the bond market. People have responded to this global uncertainty by buying fixed income and that has forced the yield way down on these bonds.

First, it's important for people to know that when the price of a bond goes up, the yield goes down. So you'll see bonds now, low-quality, risky bonds not investment-grade bonds – trading at prices way above par so that their yields are actually less than 5%. It's absolutely insane to purchase these low-quality bonds. You know through history that more than 5% of these bonds are likely to default.

If you bought a broad portfolio of these low-quality bonds trading around par, over time you would make nothing. Meanwhile, over a 10-year period, the purchasing power of the dollar is going to decline by 15% or 20%, even if we're wrong about any kind of crisis.

The simple reality is that you're going to lose money in real terms with these bonds, but most people don't understand that.

Something else you want to be cautious about is life-insurance policies. If you have an insurance policy you've been paying for a long time and the death benefit isn't likely to be paid until 20-25 years from now... the real value of that payout is nothing compared with the value that you are giving the insurance companies. The insurance companies got pre-inflation dollars, and they only have to pay out post-inflation dollars.

Instead of buying life insurance, buy the life-insurance company instead, right? If it can afford to pay out those benefits, it's not doing it for free. It's getting something more out of the deal. So watch out for these bonds that trade at or above par, especially long-term bonds. Watch out for insurance policies.

Stansberry Research: What about specific types of companies that you should own?

Porter: A lot of people want to buy mining companies as a shield against inflation. They think, "I'll go buy a gold mine and if inflation drives up the price of gold, I'll be protected."

But the reality is these companies don't tend to perform well during periods of inflation. It costs them more to replace their production than they're able to earn selling their gold.

Think about this for a second... say a gold mine has $100 million of gold in it. And you buy it with today's dollars. You're only going to get paid for your gold in the inflated currency. Now, you'll get paid more for it. But in terms of real purchasing power, there's no great increase.

And what happens when the $100 million is gone when all the gold has been produced?

Stansberry Research: There's nothing left.

Porter: Exactly. You own nothing.

So in 10 years, you've got nothing but some inflated dollars back. Meanwhile, what really happens is the manager of the gold mine says, "We need to find a new resource." He takes all the money he made selling the gold and buys another hugely expensive mine. And the shareholder gets nothing.

Stansberry Research: What about asset-rich companies that aren't mines or resource-producing companies? Something like a real estate trust or something along those lines.

Porter: What you really want to do is focus on what we call "beachfront property." Not literally beachfront property... but the best assets in the world. You want to focus on what we call "Trophy Assets" that can't be replicated.

The key is you've got to make sure you don't pay too much for it because the prices of these asset prices will soar in anticipation of inflation. And we've already seen that in real estate. The great example of this is the Empire State Building went public in 2013.

Stansberry Research: Wow, I didn't know that.

Porter: Yeah. So think about this for a second. Are the folks who own the Empire State Building likely to know more or less about the real estate market than the general public?

So when you see that kind of thing, you have to be very, very cautious. Likewise, the best portfolio ever assembled of corporate real estate was a business called Equity Office Properties.

A famous Chicagoan named Sam Zell built that business over a 30-year period. Sam is one of the people we quote warning about the potential for the loss of the world reserve currency. And Sam sold all of his real estate in January 2007. He sold the company he spent his life assembling, and he did it because people's expectations of inflation were even greater than the risks of inflation.

And so you have to warn people that this Trophy Asset strategy is well known, and you have to be cautious about when you decide to follow it. Our bias is you should try to buy these things when they're trading at half of whatever their estimated asset value is.

And you're only going to get those opportunities during certain rare crisis moments. You have to watch them all and be ready to acquire them at the appropriate time.

But **the best way to protect yourself from inflation is by owning your own asset-light business**. Just for a moment, imagine what would happen to our publishing company if the dollar fell by 50% overnight.

Stansberry Research: You probably wouldn't have to pay me as much.

Porter: Exactly... all of my costs would fall in real terms because all of my labor costs would be decimated. The amounts we're paying you guys in real terms would fall in half. Meanwhile, what are my real asset costs? I have almost none.

Stansberry Research: Not a bad business to be in...

Porter: That's what I want people to understand. Cutting a few costs would eliminate all of the damage of inflation to my business. And it would be great because it would reduce my labor costs tremendously.

So for folks who have the wherewithal to structure their own businesses in an asset-light basis, that's the very best way to deal with inflation.

If you can't have your own business that's asset light, you need to look in the stock market for businesses that have that characteristic. We call these "capital efficient" companies. I've written volumes and volumes and volumes about this.

We recommended Hershey in my *Investment Advisory* in December 2007, which was pretty much the worst possible time that you could imagine to buy stock, right?

It was right in front of 2008, and we didn't stop out of it – meaning it didn't drop 25% from when we purchased... which would have triggered us to sell from our portfolio. This simple fact alone tells you how resilient that business is.

I studied the price per ounce of chocolate versus the price per ounce of gold over a 100-year period. And it turns out that Hershey's chocolate bars were a better hedge against inflation than gold was. I think that's a really valuable secret.

It just goes to show you that there's a mindset out there that the only way to protect yourself against inflation is gold. That mindset is wrong. There are many consumer products that people value more than gold.

And you know I would put medicine in that category. I would put oil in that category, and I would put beloved consumer goods like Coca-Cola and chocolate in that category.

Stansberry Research: All right. Well I think we got good stuff. I think we have some really solid advice that our readers can use to their advantage.

Porter: Before you go, I just want to make one thing clear. I want people to know they shouldn't feel paranoid or scared. There's an easy, sensible strategy that will make you wealthier than you otherwise would be so long as you understand the forces at play and prepare accordingly.

Stansberry Research: Thanks again for your time, Porter.

Porter: Thank you.

– Chapter 4 –

Summary: Nine Keys to Survive a Currency Crisis

1. Have a safe place outside the bank to store a reasonable amount of currency, gold, and silver.

2. Become less "U.S.-dependent" by holding assets overseas and/or having a plan to evacuate to another country.

3. Keep a seven- to 10-day supply of cash, medicines, food, water, and guns and ammunition.

4. Find a way to get to any of the 50 or so places in the country that have real concentrations of wealth.

5. Review your critical documents (birth certificate, passport, etc.) once a year.

6. Do not hold expensive, poor-quality bonds.

7. Be cautious buying life insurance.

8. Own your own "asset-light" business.

9. Focus your stock investing on "Trophy Assets" and capital-efficient businesses.

Now, in the following sections of *The American Jubilee*, we'll review a few other methods that – when applied correctly – will help you not just survive the national crisis we see coming... but also prosper from it.

We'll look at the best commodity investment you can own to hedge against a shakeup in the financial markets. We'll look at the most profitable and stable form of leveraged investing around. We'll look at how to earn crisis-proof, inflation-proof income streams in the stock market. And I'll share my crash course on how to become a better investor.

The worst thing you can do for your future is ignore the looming Debt Jubilee. The best thing you can do is absorb the lessons we share in this book. These are some of the most valuable insights I can give you right now. This is the stuff I would want to know if our roles were reversed.

I can't guarantee that you'll make it through unscathed. But take these ideas to heart, and you'll be light years ahead of the majority of investors.

Part III

Secrets of the Silver Markets

– Chapter 1 –

Owning Silver Is the Best Decision You Can Make

If you've got the means to take a small percentage of your portfolio and put it at risk, there are several speculations that could produce life-changing gains if and when they hit...

To us, speculation has a specific meaning. Speculating is an attempt to profit from temporary market extremes. In every mania, speculators have identified distorted markets (by government actions or otherwise)... and then positioned themselves to earn massive profits when, inevitably, the market forces overwhelm third-party actions.

Just consider the 2008 financial crisis when the U.S. government – through Fannie Mae and Freddie Mac – lent to almost anyone wanting to buy a house in America. Just before the crash, the government owned or guaranteed roughly 45% of all mortgages in the U.S.

Speculators like hedge-fund manager Steve Eisman knew what was happening and took the other side of the bet. Eisman knew an epic crash was on the way and made once-in-a-lifetime gains by betting against the real estate sector. He made highly leveraged "asymmetrical" bets using securities like options and credit default swaps. These securities cost a small amount of money, but offered investors the potential to make huge sums if a wide variety of mortgages defaulted.

When the mortgage bubble burst, the default rate on mortgages hit 10% annually and more than $1 trillion defaulted. Speculators like

Eisman made billions. If stories like Steve Eisman's sound familiar, you may have read about it in the book *The Big Short*.

Now America has a new crisis emerging. We can't know exactly when the Jubilee will happen. But it is coming. And we think the damage will send the markets into a tailspin.

The rich and well-connected are going to get richer from this Jubilee. Meanwhile, the poor are going to get wiped out. The good news is you don't have to be among them. We have an easy and predictable way for you to make a heck of a lot of money.

When there is a big shakeup in the financial markets, the price of silver goes wild.

No other investment asset loves a monetary crisis like silver does.

I would urge (even beg) you to read (and reread) the May 2006 issue of *Stansberry's Investment Advisory*. It explains in great detail the reasons why silver prices tend to soar during a monetary crisis. It also explains the three phases of a monetary crisis.

Back then, I explained why we were on the cusp of entering the second phase of a monetary crisis, which I defined this way...

> Phase II happens as the government begins to take actions to halt rising prices through force. The government will not cut its own spending, which is the primary driver of inflation... It will not begin to address the unsustainable nature of entitlement spending, or the current value of its long-tail obligations...
>
> Instead of addressing the genuine causes of inflation in the United States, the government will begin to tax, regulate, and even imprison what it labels the culprits. These efforts will only exacerbate and accelerate the rise in prices... Once Phase II begins, more and more people have tangible evidence that something has gone badly wrong with the economy. They begin to hoard. Rich people hoard gold and silver.

After I wrote those words, the annual government deficit soared from less than $300 billion to around $600 billion annually. The U.S.

government continues to foster a soak-the-rich, tax-and-regulate regime, in which a dozen or more states have enacted steeply progressive "millionaire" taxes. Former President Obama personally lobbied the American people for more taxes on the "rich" – all of which were used to justify more government spending and ever-larger government deficits.

Meanwhile, the inflation and the joblessness these policies cause have led to a return to "misery index"' conditions in the United States and more social unrest. I wish I could tell you the worst was over and our leaders will soon come to their senses and return our country to sound economic policies. But that will not happen.

Instead, the political dynamic in our country – where criminals run wild on the streets (and in the halls of Congress) while the government continues to print money to pay its debts – will lead to what I call a "Phase III" monetary crisis.

In a Phase III crisis, people flee from the currency at all costs. Civil society falls apart. Cash savings are destroyed and other forms of savings that depend on a stable currency – like insurance policies – are wiped out, too. Worst of all, the monetary crisis makes it impossible for people to save or invest in America. Our standard of living and our stature in the world collapse.

That's what's going to happen. I can't tell you exactly when. But the sure way to know how bad things are getting is to watch the Treasury markets...

As long as the world continues to buy our bonds, we're safe. But a moment will arrive – and it won't be long – when investors simply refuse to own our government's debt at almost any price. *If you don't take steps right now to protect yourself, you will be wiped out when that moment arrives.*

The best thing you can do about it is to own precious metals... especially silver. Owning silver and gold gives you real money that the politicians can't devalue and will have a hard time trying to confiscate – especially if you store it overseas. I recommend silver over gold.

During the last Jubilee in the early 1970s, silver soared by more than 2,400%. And if you buy silver this time around, you'll do well, too.

If you're going to buy silver, you must understand the silver ratio...

The market for silver has two distinct phases. First, are the times when silver trades alongside gold as money.

During these periods, there's vast global demand for silver. When gold was the world's reserve currency and silver was also used as money, silver prices averaged around 1/16 the price of gold.

On the other hand, during periods where silver was "demonetized" – when it was not commonly used as money – this ratio to gold would become completely unpegged. In 1991, for example, an ounce of silver traded for only 1/100 the price of an ounce of gold.

When I first began to perceive we were in the early stages of a huge monetary crisis, I recommended readers add silver bullion to their portfolios as a hedge against the risk of hyperinflation. Back then, silver was trading at around $14. Gold was trading for around $675. Thus, the silver ratio stood at around 50. That is, silver was trading at 1/50 the price of gold.

In November 2016, gold traded for about $1,225. Silver traded around $16. Investors who took my advice and began to stockpile precious metals have done very well.

But here's the really interesting part. In 2016, the silver ratio was around 72 – even higher than it was back in 2006. But the risks of a massive inflation have grown dramatically.

I believe silver is, by far, the better buy of the two precious metals.

Silver should be trading at a ratio of 20-25. That would put silver's price somewhere around $48 per ounce to $60 per ounce.

You have a lot of ways to invest in silver... But my colleague Dr. David Eifrig has researched an excellent way that allows individuals to take physical possession of silver without paying huge markups to the spot price (like you would buying rare coins). This unique opportunity to own real, hold-in-your-hand silver doesn't require any risky leverage or buying of mining companies that may or may not be around this time next year...

— Chapter 2 —

A Silver Investment Created by the U.S. Government

More than 200 years ago, Congress designated silver as the material for the U.S.' first coin. Congress based its new dollar on the Spanish piaster, though it took its name from a German coin called the thaler.

Congress passed the U.S. Coinage Act of 1792, which laid out the specifications for all of its new coins. It set the standards we lay out in this chapter. (You'll notice the name for dimes is "dismes." That's not a typo – it's from the Latin decima.)

The highlighted coins marked in the following table are those that we've found hold the best value.

The table shows the composition of U.S. coins for nearly 200 years, until the Coinage Act of 1965 **removed most of the silver from its coins**. Half dollars changed from 90% silver to 40% silver... And other coins were 75% copper and 25% nickel.

Then in 1970, Congress pulled the remaining silver from the coins.

Eagles	$10	247 4/8 grain (16.0 g) pure or 270 grain (17.5 g) standard gold
Half Eagles	$5	123 6/8 grain (8.02 g) pure or 135 grain (8.75 g) standard gold
Quarter Eagles	$2.50	61 7/8 grain (4.01 g) pure or 67 4/8 grain (4.37 g) standard gold
Dollars or Units	$1	371 4/16 grain (24.1 g) pure or 416 grain (27.0 g) standard silver
Half Dollars	**$0.50**	**185 10/16 grain (12.0 g) pure or 208 grain (13.5 g) standard silver**
Quarter Dollars	**$0.25**	**92 13/15 grain (6.01 g) pure or 104 grain (6.74 g) standard silver**
Dismes	**$0.10**	**37 2/16 grain (2.41 g) pure or 41 3/5 grain (1.35 g) standard silver**
Half Dismes	**$0.05**	**18 9/16 grain (1.20 g) pure or 20 4/5 grain (1.35 g) standard silver**
Cents	$0.01	11 pennyweights (17.1 g) of copper
Half Cents	$0.005	5 1/2 pennyweights (8.55 g) of copper

* 28.34 grams = 1 ounce

Coins dated before 1965 are known as "junk silver." They get tagged as "junk" because they have no value to collectors. They circulated widely in pockets and purses and show a lot of wear. By one estimate, more than 13 billion of these coins are spread around the country.

But what's bad for collectors is great for us as investors.

Because they don't have collectible value, these coins can be purchased at just a few percentage points above the spot price for an ounce of silver.

That's significant since collectible and uncirculated silver coins often have premiums of 25%-50% or more than the spot price.

How do you buy it? Junk silver comes in $1,000 face-value bags of either dimes, quarters, or half dollars. So the breakdown of a bag could be any of the following three:

- 10,000 dimes

- 4,000 quarters

- 2,000 half-dollars

Regardless of which denomination you choose, the amount of silver you are buying is the same... about 715-720 ounces.

The retail price for a $1,000 face-value bag of dimes, quarters, or half dollars in 2016 was about $13,400, plus shipping and insurance (which vary depending upon the delivery location, usually ranging from $60-$120).

So let's say the total cost is about $13,500. (By the way, many dealers will split bags into smaller bags to fit your budget.)

Now, take $13,500 and divide it by 10,000 dimes and you get real, hold-in-your-hand silver for just $1.35. (Keep in mind, this value can fluctuate daily with the price of silver and with demand.) And that's why we say you can get silver for less than $3.

As the price and demand for silver increase, so will the value of your "junk silver."

But remember, silver is volatile. Any change in the price of silver could change your total cost.

Plus, growing demand will push up dealer premiums on junk silver, further multiplying your gains.

In addition to the discount you can get buying junk silver, you have four other reasons to own these coins rather than bullion, exchange-traded funds, mining stocks, or collectible coins:

90% of silver coins are well recognized – These coins are already well known. The fact is, you rarely find them in day-to-day circulation because people have already gone through their change looking for these valuable coins. And as precious-metal demand increases, even more people will recognize the coins.

90% of silver coins are easily divisible – Unlike a silver bar or gold coin, junk silver coins are already portioned in smaller amounts should you ever need to use them in everyday transactions.

90% of silver coins are liquid – There has always been a demand for these types of coins. Thanks to a dealer network and places like eBay, plenty of buyers are available should you ever want to cash in your gains.

90% of silver coins do not require verification – The silver content of these coins is so widely understood, you don't need to verify the authenticity and value. Again, there's no collectible value, and everyone understands they're 90% silver.

— Chapter 3 —

Safe Silver: A Far Better Business

"Junk silver" is an excellent way to protect against a currency crisis.

But to capture greater gains as panicked investors rush to bullion, I like to own silver companies. Silver companies follow the movement of the underlying metal while also providing leverage. If we own silver bullion, we only make the price increase of silver. If we own a silver company, we can earn much, much more.

Wheaton Precious Metals (NYSE: WPM) is the largest silver streamer in the world.

A "streamer" is essentially a company that purchases the silver (or gold) byproduct from base-metal miners. Simply put, when a copper miner (or zinc miner or iron miner) extracts ore from his mine, that rock likely includes a lot of minerals other than copper – including silver. The copper miner doesn't want the hassle of smelting and dealing with the silver from his mine.

Approximately 70% of the world's silver is produced as a byproduct from other metal mines... So a silver streamer, like Wheaton, is there to take it off his hands.

Wheaton will swoop in and make a deal upfront for the silver. It's a good deal for the base-metal miner because he gets guaranteed income for his silver. And it's a great deal for Wheaton because it gets a guaranteed supply of silver without the hassles and risks of actually mining it.

Wheaton has dozens of long-term agreements across 28 gold and silver mining assets with companies like Barrick, Goldcorp, and Vale.

Wheaton's streaming agreements are forecast to produce about 28 million ounces of silver and 340,000 ounces of gold for full-year 2017. The company expects to continue at that level of production through 2020.

To understand exactly how these deals work, let's look at Wheaton's agreement at Peñasquito, the second-largest mine in Mexico. It's a world-class gold/silver/lead/zinc deposit.

Wheaton's flagship deal is an agreement with Goldcorp for 25% of the silver produced at the Peñasquito mine... for the life of the mine. This is the largest silver deposit in the world. Even a 25% stake ranks among the planet's top 20 silver deposits.

In April 2007, Wheaton paid Goldcorp $485 million. Since 2010, silver production at Peñasquito averaged 6 million ounces per year. In the past few years, it's up to 7 million.

The company expects to sell around 7 million ounces of silver from Peñasquito for an average price of $16 per ounce. With silver trading around $17 per ounce and the average cash cost per ounce less than $5, the company's profit is more than $12 per ounce.

Wheaton's fundamentals are nearly perfect... It has reasonable debt levels, hundreds of millions of ounces of silver equivalent reserves, an operating margin of around 31%, and a secure cash flow from mines scattered around the globe. For the 12 months ended September 30, 2017, the company generated $545 million in FCF.

Wheaton Precious Metals' strategy has paid off so far... but its results will get even better as the price of silver rises.

Wheaton's costs are fixed. So as with the Peñasquito example, any increase in the silver price goes straight to its net profit. According to the company's November 2017 presentation, it expects to pay an average of $4.71 per ounce for the silver it receives for the 2017 to 2021 period.

If you look at Wheaton's share price compared with its earnings, you'll see a direct relationship to the price of silver. In other words, as the silver price goes up, people will pay more for the stock.

That means a rise in the silver price gives your investment "juice."

Of course, the leverage works both ways. When the metal sells off, so do the shares in Wheaton.

When investing in trophy-asset companies like Wheaton Precious Metals, we like to compare the company's market cap with the value of its tangible assets. Our aim is to buy a company when its market cap trades at a discount to its tangible assets. At least 25%... higher if possible.

We've analyzed Wheaton's numbers going back to 2005. In February 2016, there was a brief window to purchase the stock at a discount. The last time you could buy the company at a discount to total assets before that was in October and November 2008.

During that time, you could have bought the company for up to a 30% discount to total assets. The stock soared from lows around $3 per share at that time to as high as $47 in early 2011 when silver was also trading at multiyear highs of about $48 per ounce.

As of December 31, 2016, the company's total assets equaled $6.1 billion. The company carries no goodwill or intangible assets on its balance sheet, so we'll use its total assets valuation. As we go to press in late 2017, the company's market cap sits around $9.2 billion. That's a 34% premium based on its total assets valuation.

But remember this: **From 2004 to 2016, total assets grew from $157 million to $6.1 billion**. That's massive growth in 12 years. Now, we don't expect growth to continue at such high rates. But looking at the past five years of data, the company still enjoyed an impressive 36% annual growth rate.

Given the price action in the precious metals market and the company's ability to grow assets, we believe you'll get another opportunity to buy at a discount.

Part IV

How to Own the World's Trophy Assets

– Chapter 1 –

The Most Profitable and Stable Form of Leveraged Investing

In mid-2007, private-equity firm Blackstone Group (NYSE: BX) went public in a huge and highly publicized initial stock offering.

The public was so eager to buy the stock, bankers were able to push the value of the firm to nearly $40 billion. Blackstone had roughly 1,500 employees at the time. According to the stock market, these employees were worth $26.6 million each, making them the most valuable people in the history of capitalism... at least, for a few months.

Due to the outrageous valuation and the incredible hype, the stock soon cratered. It fell from more than $30 per share to less than $5 in a little more than a year. We wrote at the time of the IPO that Blackstone's shares were not safe. We saw the IPO as one of the most obvious signs of a general stock market peak...

> Chief Executive Stephen Schwarzman and his partner Peter Peterson started this company in 1985 with $400,000. They've worked hard for 22 years. And they're no dummies. They've seen a top in the credit markets before... and this time they're cashing out.
>
> – *The Stansberry Digest, June 17, 2007*

The Blackstone IPO turned out to be the metaphoric bell ringing at the top of the credit/housing/stock market bubble of 2004-2008. Within only a few weeks of the IPO, the credit markets began to crater, making it harder and more expensive for private-equity firms like Blackstone to get the financing they needed for their deals. Within a few months, credit was simply not available at any price. The stock's share price collapsed.

It would be easy to write off the success of the private-equity funds in the 1990s and early 2000s as simply an aberration – part of the excesses created by a credit-fueled bull market. Except that Blackstone survived the crash.

Blackstone didn't just survive... It prospered and became even larger, in terms of assets under management. At more than $30 billion in market cap, investors value the firm at around $13 million per employee in 2016. With $361 billion in assets under management and $4.4 billion in revenue in 2016, these folks are still incredibly good at making money.

Blackstone's survival, even more than its earlier success, argues its strategy is no fluke. Its acumen is real.

Whatever your particular opinion about Blackstone's future is, you can't deny the private-equity model has proven to be the most profitable and stable form of leveraged investing. In the Securities and Exchange Commission filings that accompanied the IPO, Blackstone disclosed that, while still a private company, its co-founder Stephen Schwarzman earned more than $300 million a year in compensation.

These numbers and the success of so many of Blackstone's investments raise the question...

How do they do it?

How does Blackstone make so much money with so few people? And what can we learn from its success?

– Chapter 2 –

How Private Equity Works

Private-equity firms are mysterious and often portrayed in the liberal media as sinister. Few investors understand how they work.

But everyone knows one thing: They make a lot of money. *On average, Blackstone's clients have earned about 22% annually from their investments in Blackstone's private-equity funds since the firm's inception in the 1980s.*

That's after accounting for the firm's 2% annual management fee and the 20% of profits it takes as its carried interest.

The clients are happy to pay those fees because that 22% rate of return doubles their money in a little more than three years. These kinds of returns aren't normally available to equity investors. Even Warren Buffett, the greatest investor who ever lived, has only averaged about 20% over the long term.

How do they do it?

Simple: They borrow money. Private-equity firms use other people's money to buy assets. Then they use the earnings from those assets to pay back the debt. After a few years, they're left owning the assets outright and can sell them back to the public via a new IPO. In short... they engineer deals that enable them to transform debt into equity.

That might sound complicated, but it's not.

It's essentially the same thing that mom-and-pop real estate investors do all the time. They buy a house, putting only 20% down in equity. They get a bank to loan them the balance, using the asset (the house) as collateral. Then they find a renter to pay the interest and the principal (by renting the house).

After a while – usually seven to 10 years – the mortgage is gone. The owners, who only paid 20% of the initial cost, are able to sell the property to a new buyer for more than they paid, resulting in a huge gain.

Private-equity firms do the same thing, using stocks instead of houses.

Like real estate investors, they start by searching for assets that are "diamonds in the rough" – companies that are managing their assets poorly and/or have seen their shares badly mispriced by the market.

Then, using good contacts and relationships with the major commercial and investment banks, they raise colossal amounts of credit, borrowing billions to buy the companies they target. A lot of the big takeover deals you see written about in the papers are private-equity deals. A typical private-equity fund will buy around 20 different companies over seven years.

But... chances are good that you've never been invited to invest in a private-equity fund.

These pools of capital typically only serve very high net-worth individuals and large institutions, like sovereign-wealth funds, pension funds, and insurance companies.

To see how a private-equity deal really works, from start to finish, let's look at an actual deal...

Back in 2006, Richard Kinder, the Chairman of Kinder Morgan (NYSE: KMI), the huge natural gas and oil pipeline company, was frustrated with his company's share price.

The firm had added billions in assets, via a new pipeline constructed under the Rocky Mountains. Yet the stock market didn't seem to notice. Kinder told his investors on a conference call in April 2006 that, at that current price, he'd like to own a lot more of the company. (He held 18% at the time.)

He meant what he said. He called his bankers at Goldman Sachs, who organized a group of private-equity funds (led by the Carlyle Group) to buy the company for $15 billion. To raise the money, the Carlyle Group tapped the banks it had worked with over many years. Since Kinder already owned 18% of the company, the private-equity firms borrowed something on the order of $10 billion.

Nothing really changed about the company, its employees, or its management team. Kinder is one of the true titans of the energy industry. A bunch of guys from New York weren't going to tell him how to do his job better.

But by only putting up $3 billion in equity to buy the company... the private-equity fund was positioning itself to make a windfall return. That is, it invested $3 billion to get a business that was already worth $13 billion, not including Kinder's stake.

The company – not the private-equity funds – then spent the next few years paying down its debts and growing its pipelines. By the end of 2009, the long-term debt was down to only $2.7 billion. And in early 2011, the stock was again sold to the public. Investors paid $30 a share, valuing the business at $21 billion.

The private-equity firms took $3 billion and turned it into roughly $15 billion in a little less than six years. Richard Kinder ended up with 30% of the company, which he kept. And the private-equity investors made five times their money. Plus, the company paid them roughly $1 billion a year in dividends along the way.

Look at the math: The private-equity firms bought a company from other investors worth $13 billion (with $3 billion of their cash and shares and $10 billion in bank debt). Then, thanks to growing earnings and a few acquisitions, they paid themselves roughly $6 billion in dividends (which doubled their money) before selling the entity back to the public for $21 billion.

Did you follow what happened? The answer is, almost nothing changed in terms of the company or its operations. The only thing that changed was the firm's capital structure. **A lot of debt was**

added and this capital flowed through the company and into the hands of the shareholders.

It's a great deal, eh? Too bad we can't invest the same way, right? Well... what if we could?

– Chapter 3 –

Private-Equity-Like Stocks

We have a few obvious ways to invest in private-equity deals. The simplest thing to do is buy the private-equity firms, many of which went public following Blackstone's 2007 IPO.

In fact, the stocks of private-equity companies like Blackstone Group and Kohlberg Kravis Roberts (NYSE: KKR) are some of our favorite equities in the market. Thanks to the Federal Reserve's loose-money policies, they're in their "sweet spot."

They have nearly unlimited access to cheap capital, thanks to falling interest rates and the increasing money supply. This allows them to finance bigger and bigger deals – or in Blackstone's case, unload assets at rich multiples to their original prices.

And as the world's central banks continue to create trillions of dollars of paper money, private-equity firms gather more and more assets.

To take advantage of private-equity deals, you could also buy the shares of the companies private-equity firms are selling back to the public. The firms typically hold their stakes in these companies for several years. Often enough, these stocks perform well because they're highly leveraged, well-managed, and pay big dividends.

But a third way to invest in private-equity deals holds even more promise...

There is a group of companies whose assets are so valuable that they always have access to the credit markets. **We call them "trophy assets."**

These companies own one-of-a-kind assets. When managed the right way, they give public market investors the same high returns as private-equity investors because they can be safely leveraged to produce high returns on equity. While we wouldn't recommend investing in highly leveraged stocks in most cases... there are some important exceptions. Some assets are of such high quality, they always have access to debt financing.

For example, take the most valuable mine in the world – the Grasberg complex in Papua, Indonesia.

Discovered in the late 1930s and developed by the Rockefeller family in the 1960s, the mining district began producing copper, gold, and silver in the early 1970s. In 2014, the mine is still the world's largest source of copper (averaging 1 billion pounds a year over the past five years) and gold (averaging 1.6 million ounces a year over the past five years).

The mine is so valuable, its eventual discovery was among the motivations that led the Japanese to invade the South Pacific. Likewise, when the Rockefellers' interest in the mine was threatened in the 1960s, the U.S. government engineered a civil war in Indonesia. The coup included one of the largest mass killing sprees in history, which followed a CIA-orchestrated revolution in September 1965.

A reliable death toll number has never been published, but eyewitnesses claim at least 1 million people were murdered in Indonesia. The number of floating corpses seriously impeded the country's river traffic. One of the first major acts of the new government was to annex Papua and take control of the mine.

Despite its bloody political origins, the mine itself is a stupendous human achievement. It sits among the highest mountain peaks in the world (more than 14,000 feet high) in one of the most remote places on Earth. Grasberg is a gigantic open-pit mine, with a mile-wide crater, which can be seen from space.

The facility also includes the world's largest milling equipment, which can process 240,000 metric tons of ore per day. The ore is sent via a slurry pipeline that runs more than 70 miles through the jungle to a seaport built to serve the mine.

Grasberg is a global trophy asset, perhaps the single-greatest trophy asset in the world.

Ownership is split between the Indonesian government (which controls 10%) and the public investors of global mining giant Freeport-McMoRan (NYSE: FCX), which owns 90%. The company estimates the mine still contains 30 billion pounds of copper, 30 million ounces of gold, and 113 million ounces of silver.

Now, you should know that Freeport-McMoRan has found itself in the midst of some hot-button issues, including a labor strike in 2011. And as recently as 2014, the company was mired in a spat with the Indonesian government over taxes. But the assets are there, and Freeport-McMoRan owns 90% of them.

Investors willing to buy at the right price and ride out the volatility will do well.

The gold alone would be worth around $38 billion at 2017 prices. Given the copper and silver resource in the ore, the gold could certainly be mined for free.

Interestingly, though... the company's market cap is only about $20 billion. The discount to the company's obvious asset value isn't unusual. In fact, Freeport-McMoRan is one of the more volatile stocks we regularly follow. The value of its assets changes slowly. (In general, the value rises thanks to the impact of inflation.) But its share price bounces all around.

For example, in 2008, Freeport-McMoRan shares fell from $60 all the way down to almost $10 – a collapse of almost 80%. You can bet nothing changed about the Grasberg mine during that year. All that copper, gold, and silver was still sitting there, roasting under the equatorial sun.

Folks who claim that the stock market is perfectly efficient... that there are never important discrepancies between the price of a stock and the value of the underlying asset... should spend some time watching this stock. It often shows huge discrepancies between share price and asset value.

And as you'll see in the next chapter, that's exactly what we're looking for...

– Chapter 4 –

To Maximize Your Returns, Buy Right

To replicate the returns of private equity, our strategy is simply to buy the highest-quality assets in the world – assets that can safely carry a lot of debt – when those assets are trading at a broad discount to both their historic valuation and their proven tangible asset value.

In essence, **we want to buy the Hope Diamond... but only at a cubic zirconia-like price**. The discounted price alone assures us of a good return over time. But there's something else that will help us make even more money... leverage. The quality of the assets these kinds of companies hold allows them to safely employ a lot of debt, which greatly boosts returns.

Take MGM Resorts International (NYSE: MGM), for example. The company owns most of the Las Vegas strip, including half of CityCenter, a $9 billion hotel and casino development.

CityCenter was at one point the largest privately financed development in the history of the United States.

MGM owns a host of similar, one-of-a-kind properties in the world's leading gambling cities, including Macau, the only place in China where gambling is legal.

According to the company's accountants, its properties are worth "only" $15 billion. It's important to realize that these balance sheet valuations almost always significantly understate the actual current market value because most of these assets are kept on the books at their acquisition cost.

MGM's assets may be worth more than the $15 billion accounting "acquisition cost." MGM's assets on the Vegas strip include the Bellagio, MGM Grand Las Vegas, The Mirage, Mandalay Bay, Luxor, New York-New York, Monte Carlo, Excalibur, and Circus Circus Las Vegas... nearly 3.3 million square feet on the strip.

It also owns resorts and casinos in other regions in the U.S. including Atlantic City, Detroit, and Mississippi as well as 56% of MGM Macau in China.

Collectively, MGM's properties contain 47,540 hotel rooms and close to 26,000 slot machines in operation.

Consider that in 2009 (in the middle of one of the biggest Vegas recessions in history), MGM sold its Treasure Island casino on the strip for nearly $14,000 per square foot. At those prices, MGM's Vegas strip properties are worth more than $46 billion all by themselves... You get the Macau property and the other U.S. property for nearly nothing.

Against its assets, MGM has borrowed $13 billion. For many companies, this would be too much debt... But MGM can easily afford the $800 million it pays in interest because the quality of its assets is so high.

In a few years, the company could pay down these debts, leaving investors with massive increases to equity. Now, the company may not do this. It could buy additional assets, instead (more likely). **But the point is, as long as interest rates are so low, the company gets to use this capital for next to nothing, which means its shareholders are going to get rich.**

It's the same thing private-equity investors do: They convert debt into profit.

So... how much should you pay to own almost all of the Las Vegas strip... and a bunch of other first-class properties in the world's gambling centers? How much would you pay for the equity, knowing its growth potential? Well... you might be surprised.

The stock fell from almost $100 per share to less than $10 during the crisis of 2008. Again, nothing much changed about its business. Its hotels are still one-of-a-kind. They are still full of gamblers. And last time I checked, Vegas is still there.

What changes, as you know, is the market's appreciation of these assets. But the assets themselves don't change much. They can always be used as collateral. They always turn a profit. MGM proved this by surviving the crisis.

– Chapter 5 –

Why This Kind of Investing Is So Profitable

Trophy asset investing is special for two reasons.

First, unlike a lot of other investments, you can know what these assets are worth because they always carry a premium value to comparable properties thanks to their prized nature.

We could spend years trying to figure out what, say, Google, is really worth. And we might never figure it out... But with companies that hold trophy assets, we can know with tremendous confidence that the underlying assets are always going to be worth a lot.

And that brings us to the second key part of the strategy: **high returns on equity, thanks to leverage.**

Financing for these kinds of assets is always available. That enables the companies that own these assets to use a lot of debt to increase their annual returns on equity, which is exactly the same thing that private-equity firms do. That's why the ongoing profits from holding these stocks can be so high. This is what gives us our biggest advantage.

Private-equity firms earn high returns by taking big risks. They manage those risks by playing an active role in managing the businesses they buy.

Since we're public investors and don't have a voice in the day-to-day operations of the companies we own, we can only invest in highly leveraged companies when we are certain the underlying assets are of the highest quality. By limiting ourselves to watching only the highest-quality companies, we greatly reduce our risk.

Here's a list of stocks that qualify as bona-fide trophy properties...

Rank	Company	Sym	Trophy Asset	Mkt Cap^	Total Assets^	(Disc) / Prem to Total Assets	% Above Low Valuation
1	Facebook (1)	FB	Social network	$521.6	$79.0	560%	38%
2	Union Pacific	UNP	Railroads	$91.3	$57.4	59%	70%
3	Rio Tinto	RIO	Commodities	$86.0	$90.9	-5%	16%
4	American Tower	AMT	Communications towers	$62.7	$32.3	94%	60%
5	Freeport-McMoran	FCX	Copper and gold mine	$20.2	$37.3	-46%	23%
6	BHP Billiton	BHP	Commodities	$103.8	$117.0	-11%	13%
7	Royal Gold	RGLD	Gold royalties	$5.6	$3.1	82%	46%
8	Empire State Realty Trust	ESRT	Empire State Building	$3.3	$3.8	-15%	46%
9	Posco	PKX	Steel	$25.0	$69.9	-64%	39%
10	Walt Disney	DIS	Theme parks	$158.6	$95.8	66%	63%
11	Enterprise Products Partners	EPD	Energy pipelines	$52.9	$53.3	-1%	43%
12	Boston Properties	BXP	Office and retail space - Boston	$19.2	$19.3	0%	75%
13	Wheaton Precious Metals	WPM	Silver royalties	$9.1	$5.9	53%	19%
14	Weyerhaeuser	WY	Timber	$27.3	$18.4	48%	73%
15	MGM	MGM	Casinos	$18.8	$29.1	-35%	56%
16	Cresud	CRESY	Farmland	$1.1	$14.5	-93%	2%
17	Potash	POT	Fertilizer mines	$16.0	$17.4	-8%	3%
18	Kinder Morgan	KMI	Energy pipelines	$38.1	$80.4	-53%	16%
19	Sinclair Broadcast	SBGI	Spectrum	$3.3	$6.7	-50%	43%
20	Franco-Nevada	FNV	Precious metal royalties	$15.0	$4.7	216%	93%
21	Calpine	CPN	Power generation	$5.4	$16.8	-68%	44%
22	Targa Resources	TRGP	Energy pipelines	$9.2	$14.0	-34%	60%
23	Teekay LNG	TGP	LNG Fleet	$1.4	$4.6	-70%	24%
24	Transocean	RIG	Offshore Rigs	$4.0	$22.4	-82%	2%

^ All amounts in billions U.S. dollars
(1) Portfolio holding

As you can see, many of these firms are in the natural resource industry. There was a huge bull market in resources for 14 years. Many modern investors don't believe these "Hope Diamonds" will ever trade at cubic-zirconia prices. But trust us... they will.

As a general rule of thumb, **we want to wait to buy these stocks when we can get at least a 25% discount from tangible asset value.** (There are a few exceptions, which we'll explain.) The larger the discount, the more interested we become. Keep in mind, 25% is a broad guideline, not an automatic "buy" trigger.

When we see one of these companies trading at that size discount, we must evaluate the individual stock before making specific buying recommendations. In some circumstances, we may demand an even larger discount...

This kind of investing is a little like buying real estate. As good real estate investors know, you're buying "location" – the quality of the property – not countertops or flooring. All of the cosmetic stuff can be fixed.

We will focus on two key variables: **First, we need to understand a lot about the history of the stock price relative to the value of the tangible assets the company owns.**

Obviously, we want to buy these assets at the biggest possible discount. But in some cases, that's not possible. So *we need to make sure that in the context of the company's trading history, we're buying at the right time.*

Second, we have to make sure nothing is fundamentally wrong with the assets we're buying. To make sure they're not impaired, we look at the current return on equity. This gives us a good indication about the future rate of return. Ideally, we want to see annual returns on equity of 20% or more... as our plan is to make about 20% annually.

To do that, we've got to buy the world's best assets when they trade at a significant discount. Leverage will help us too, as it will ramp up the returns on equity.

The hard part is, the companies with the best annualized return on equity are normally going to trade at a big premium to asset value. We're looking for outliers... stocks with great assets and a great return on equity but that trade at huge discounts to asset value.

Looking at the previous summary table, you can immediately see several companies trading at a substantial discount to tangible asset value. But to decide if any represent good investing opportunities, we start by comparing the size of the discount to the return on equity. That shows you where you can get the best quality and the biggest discount.

Below, you'll find a comparison of the individual stocks in this report across two variables: discount to asset value (price) and return on equity (quality).

This regression chart plots individual "trophy asset" stocks across two variables: our valuation ranking and our overall financial strength ranking.

The valuation ranking is based on how cheap each company's discount or premium to asset value (price) is today compared with its lowest valuation in the last 10 years.

The financial strength ranking is based on our proprietary scoring system, which uses many key financial ratios and metrics to determine the overall health of each business.

The chart compares each company's valuation ranking with its financial strength ranking.

Great opportunities don't come around every day. That's why we've built this screen... to monitor the companies with the world's most prized assets so we can buy them when the market loses sight of what they're really worth. You can't always buy the Hope Diamond at a cubic-zirconia price. But when you can, it's an exceptional opportunity...

Just remember: With this kind of investing, you make your money based on when you buy. As a general rule... Buy these stocks when they trade for less than 75% of asset value (said another way, at a 25% discount to asset value) and when a confirmed uptrend is in place.

Waiting on the trend to turn in the right direction is important because we've seen in the past that the market participants will often dump these asset-rich companies at prices that don't make any sense. We want to wait for that irrational selling to subside and buy when the shares are on their way back up... as opposed to trying to catch a "falling knife."

Doing so will produce profits of more than 20% a year. And the best part is... it's not hard. All you have to do is follow a few of the world's best assets. Then buy them when they're trading at huge discounts to their underlying values.

Part V

Porter Stansberry's Crash
Course on How to Become
a Better Investor

– Chapter 1 –

The Fed's Biggest Fear Should Be Yours, Too

My crash course to become a better investor is composed of 10 critical lessons that show you how to make big returns while taking minimal risk.

The lessons cover topics such as...

- The seven best "one click" funds to manage your portfolio.

- The only sector I hope my children invest in.

- Four steps to consistently beat the market.

- The trick to safely produce triple-digit winners in the market.

- An easy test to find great investments.

You might not agree with all these ideas. But I promise they will encourage you to think about investing in a new way... and the knowledge you'll gain will last your entire life.

———————•———————

We'll start off with a topic that I bet will surprise you... a review of the world's best exchange-traded funds (ETFs).

I'm going to give you seven well-run ETFs that you can buy safely and enjoy their outstanding investment performance... even if you know absolutely nothing about investing and you have no desire to learn. This is for all of our readers who don't want to manage their own assets, but want better-than-reasonable returns on their savings.

ETFs are investment funds that can hold any of a variety of assets (like stocks, but also bonds or commodities). The key feature is their shares trade on public stock exchanges, so you can buy shares of them just as you would shares of an individual company's stock.

What we're looking for in our list of the seven best ETFs isn't necessarily diversification or the cheapest possible fees... We're looking for funds that help investors succeed. We're looking for funds that are based on solid financial research and follow strategies that make sense to us.

Most investors don't know this, but most of the money that goes into index funds and ETFs ends up being managed around the basis of the S&P 500 Index. That index, maintained by credit-rating giant Standard & Poor's, isn't designed to help investors. It's designed to help sell S&P's bond ratings to issuers – i.e. large public companies.

The index is "weighted" toward the stocks with the largest market caps. Funds copying this index put most of their capital into the largest and most expensive stocks. That just doesn't make sense. They are literally deciding to "buy high" instead of trying to find smart ways to "buy low." Also, there's little indication of the overall quality of the business. Bigger isn't necessarily better.

Let's jump in...

No. 1: Cambria Shareholder Yield Fund (SYLD)

The basic idea here is simple... instead of buying the entire S&P 500, our friend, fund manager Meb Faber, has organized an ETF that owns nearly equal stakes in the top 100 highest "shareholder yield" stocks in the U.S.

The list is determined by looking at the market cap (the value of all outstanding shares) and the combined value of the capital the company has returned to shareholders through dividends and share buybacks.

Over time, this keeps investors' capital in the stocks that are treating their shareholders best and that are fairly priced. Cambria Shareholder Yield Fund trailed the S&P 500 in 2015 and 2016. But assuming nothing material changes with the structure of the fund over the long term, it should outperform the S&P 500. For the best results, the key is to buy when volatility strikes and the fund sells off like we saw during the first half of 2016.

Cambria Shareholder Yield Fund (SYLD) vs. S&P 500

No. 2: WisdomTree Emerging Markets Equity Fund (DEM)

The approach here is similar to Meb's SYLD. But instead of investing in large-cap U.S. stocks that treat shareholders well, DEM owns the top 100 highest-yielding emerging-market stocks. Its top holding in mid-2014? Russia's huge natural gas company Gazprom (4.7% of the portfolio).

Investing in emerging markets is hard because of the huge volatility, the poor disclosure, and the difficulty transacting in foreign markets. The key to buying funds like this is to wait until they are down substantially from previous highs. Buying these markets when nobody else wants them is when you'll do the best. Then you just sit back and wait.

This fund allows you to own a huge basket of only the best emerging-market stocks. And it pays a large dividend to reward you while you wait out the volatility. Companies in the index are weighted based on actual cash dividends paid.

No. 3: U.S. Commodity Index Fund (USCI)

You've got to be very careful when you buy a commodity fund, like the U.S. Oil Fund (USO) or the U.S. Natural Gas Fund (UNG). These ETFs sometimes do a terrible job of converting gains in commodity prices to profits for investors. That's because they invest in futures contracts on their specific commodity. So they have to roll their futures contracts forward.

These markets are often in "contango" – meaning that the forward months' prices are much higher. In these situations, the cost of rolling their contracts forward eats up all (or most) of the profits.

The U.S. Commodity Index Fund (USCI) overcomes that problem by investing in a range of different commodities – including when their forward-pricing curves are in "backwardation." That's the opposite of contango, and it allows the fund to make easy profits, even when commodity prices are flat.

The fund invests the other half of its assets in commodities whose prices are moving higher at a rapid pace. By hopping on some of these trends, the fund can still make money (most of the time) despite the contango.

You must also pay attention to the commodity cycle.

No. 4: Blackstone Mortgage Trust (BXMT)

OK, this one is not really an ETF... It's a mortgage real estate investment trust (REIT), meaning it's a business that invests in mortgages. But it might as well be an ETF...

It's managed by Blackstone, whose real-estate head (Jonathan Gray) is the most impressive Wall Street executive I've ever met.

This is a leveraged fund that invests only in top-shelf commercial properties by owning their mortgages. It does so in a unique way that eliminates the big risks faced by most leveraged mortgage REITs.

Unlike residential real estate, commercial property has little pre-payment risk. So the fund is able to lock in its interest-rate spread by using both floating-rate financing and floating-rate mortgages.

The Blackstone Mortgage Trust is about 25% less volatile than the market as a whole. That means when stocks fall, this fund tends to fall less. Likewise, when the market has a big up day, these stocks typically don't jump as much.

In my experience, investors tend to overestimate their own risk tolerance. Having low- and super-low-volatility positions is the key to building a portfolio most investors are happy with.

From 2011 to 2016, the total return for the fund (including dividends) was 225%. That equates to almost roughly 26% annualized. By comparison, the return for the S&P 500 over the same period was about 110% (16% annualized). In November 2017, the fund yielded nearly 8%.

No. 5. PowerShares KBW Property & Casualty Insurance Fund (KBWP)

Adding an insurance ETF gives you something important for your portfolio: a low-volatility way to beat the market.

We greatly prefer the property and casualty insurance business to the life insurance business because everyone dies. But not everyone wrecks their car or files a homeowners' insurance claim. As a result, property and casualty companies with excellent underwriting discipline can be outstanding investments, far better than life insurance companies.

High-quality insurance stocks produce slow and steady gains. And like the Blackstone Mortgage Trust Fund, the PowerShares KBW Property & Casualty Insurance Fund is less volatile than the overall S&P 500.

Meanwhile, the annual returns including dividends (around 17% per year from 2011 to 2016 compared with 14% for the S&P 500) are likely to continue beating the market.

No. 6: PowerShares International Dividend Achievers (PID)

This ETF owns 100 of the highest-yielding international stocks that have shares listed on one of the major global exchanges. It weights its fund into the highest-yielding stocks.

By sticking with only companies paying a good dividend and trading on major exchanges, a lot of the risk of buying foreign stocks has been removed. Also, by holding 100 companies, it offers plenty of diversification. The weighting toward higher dividends should help produce index-beating results over time.

Oil and gas make up 12% of the fund. These holdings weighed on the fund's overall performance after oil prices dropped by half from 2014 to 2016. In November 2017, PID's average price-to-earnings (P/E) ratio was 14 times earnings. By comparison, the S&P 500's P/E ratio was around 22. The dividend yield on the fund was 3.8%.

Like so many of these funds, the secret is to buy PID when it's selling cheap and nobody wants it.

No. 7: SPDR Dow Jones International Real Estate (RWX)

There's no really great international real estate ETF... yet. So in the meantime, I'd recommend just getting the broadest possible exposure to the best managers. RWX fits the bill.

Here, you're getting 100 of the biggest and best real estate firms in the world – Japan's Mitsui Fudosan, Canada's Brookfield Asset Management, Hong Kong's Link REIT, and the British Land Co. These are all legendary real estate firms... and you're getting all of them, from around the world.

From 2011 to 2016, the returns have been around 7% annually. Of course, that's less than the S&P 500, but the fund does give you exposure to some of the best investment firms in the world. And with exposure to real estate outside of the U.S., I suspect the returns here will continue to be at least as good over the next 10 years.

And if one or more of these markets take off, these firms should be among the best performers. This ETF allows us to get alongside the best firms in the business.

What you have here is a group of funds that offer you value, diversification, and smart investing strategies.

What you'll pay for these funds is next to nothing. You don't need a broker. You don't need an asset planner. You don't even need to read our newsletters (although we hope you'll do so anyway).

Put equal parts of your portfolio into these seven investment vehicles, and you'll rarely have a down quarter. Year after year, you'll beat the international stock indexes. And in almost every year, you'll beat the S&P 500.

Try to learn to allocate additional capital to this plan when other investors are panicking. But either way, learn to save something regularly – every month or every quarter at least.

My advice? Just allocate funds to whichever has performed the worst over the previous three years. If you do this for 15-20 years, I have no doubt you will end up with far more money than you ever dreamed was possible. If you do this for 30-40 years (you've got to start early), you'll end up stupendously wealthy.

There's no real trick to investing if you're disciplined enough to save and if you only buy good assets and good companies at reasonable prices. These funds enable you to do that, and do it well, in what I consider to be all of the major areas of equity finance: U.S. stocks, foreign stocks, emerging-market stocks, U.S. real estate, global real estate, commodities, and energy.

The U.S. Federal Reserve is afraid of what's going to happen to certain leveraged bond funds and other bond ETFs and mutual funds when interest rates rise (as we know they will, eventually).

Currently, bond-fund investors can withdraw their money on demand. But... just because the investors want out doesn't mean that there will be buyers (liquidity) in the market at that time. The result could be a catastrophe as bond funds show net asset values that bear no connection with reality.

Imagine that your bond fund says it's worth $30 a share, for example... but the bids on all of its portfolio holdings would only add up to, say, $25 a share. Who will take the $5 loss across $10 trillion of corporate bonds?

The answer is a hot potato. We could hear the chorus of "not me"s from hundreds of miles away. Jeremy Stein, a former Fed governor, put it this way: "It may be the essence of what shadow banking is... giving people a liquid claim on illiquid assets."

U.S. retail investors have placed more than $1 trillion into bond funds since early 2009. At the same time, broker/dealer bond inventory has fallen sharply. According to New York Fed data, bond-dealer inventories have fallen from around $260 billion in 2007 to approximately $15 billion today.

When the bond market finally rolls over, it will cause the greatest disaster in the history of finance. Think end-of-the-Roman-Empire bad. The Fed thinks some kind of fee is going to staunch the tide? No way. All we can say is that you've been warned... both by us (hundreds of times) and now by the Federal Reserve.

– Chapter 2 –

The One Business I'll Teach My Children

If you were going to limit all of your investments to only one sector of the economy – only one type of business or one kind of stock – what would you buy?

We've come to believe that, for outside and passive investors (common shareholders), only three sectors offer truly extraordinary rates of return and don't require taking *any* material risk.

Let me be clear about what I mean...

There are three sectors of the economy where companies can establish and maintain a truly *lasting* competitive advantage and where outside investors can identify attractive values.

As I teach my children about investing, I focus almost entirely on examples from these three sectors. And truly... *I spend most of my time explaining only one business to my children.*

If they come to understand this business thoroughly, I know that with a reasonable amount of saving discipline, they will be financially secure by the time they are 30 years old... and wealthy long before they reach 50.

I want to show you *why* the investment returns in these businesses are so incredibly good over the long term. I want you to know how to think about these businesses... how they work... and a few simple keys to making great investments in these sectors.

I promise... this is all far easier than you're imagining right now. Let's start with this chart...

What Kind of Business Always Beats the Market?

Source: Bloomberg

This chart shows four of the best-managed property and casualty (P&C) insurance companies in the United States.

Company No. 1 started in the 1930s insuring jitney buses and, later, long-haul truckers. In 2017, it serves niche markets and underwrites specialty insurance products. The company is worth $12 billion.

Company No. 2 got its start insuring contact lenses. In 2017, it focuses on things that other companies won't touch, like oil rigs and summer camps. It's a small public company worth $2.7 billion.

Company No. 3 was founded by a Harvard Business School graduate 50 years ago. It's still mostly a family business (even though it has public shareholders and is worth $7.3 billion). It insures almost anything commercial, from yachts to elevators.

Company No. 4 is a major global company that insures virtually anything and is worth $31 billion.

You might think that outside of being in the insurance industry, these companies have almost nothing in common. Some are small and insure essentially niche items. Others are huge, operate globally, and insure virtually anything. Yet to us, these companies look nearly the same: *They are among the best underwriters in the world.*

That means these insurance companies almost always demand more in insurance premiums than they will end up spending on insurance claims. As you will soon learn, nothing is more valuable in the financial world than having the skill and the discipline to underwrite insurance profitably.

Over the long term, all these companies have generated returns that are *more than double the S&P 500*. They did so without taking any risk. And here's the best part... their success was both *inevitable and repeatable*. These are not "lucky guesses" or fad-driven product sales.

One of our overriding goals at Stansberry Research is to give you the knowledge we'd want to have if our roles were reversed.

Knowing what I know now about finance, I wouldn't have gotten into the investment newsletter business. I would have gotten into insurance.

There is nothing more valuable that we can teach you than understanding how to invest in good P&C insurance companies. And with the legwork we do for you, it's as easy as point and click.

If a company passes our tests and you can buy it at the right price... you can be next to 100% sure that the investment will produce outstanding returns. It's like painting by numbers. Only it will make you rich.

Let me say it one more time... I believe if individuals limit themselves to only investing in P&C insurance companies, they would greatly increase their average annual returns. We don't believe that's true of any other sector of the market.

There's a simple reason for this. If you think about it for a minute, it should become intuitive... Here's why insurance is the world's best business: *Insurance is the only business in the world that enjoys a positive cost of capital.*

In every other business, companies must pay for capital. They borrow through loans. They raise equity (and pay dividends). They pay depositors. Everywhere else you look, in every other sector, in every other type of business, the cost of capital is one of the primary business considerations. Often, it's the dominant consideration.

But a well-run insurance company will routinely not only get all the capital it needs for free, *it will actually get paid to accept it.*

I want to make sure you understand this point. All the people who make their living providing financial services – banks, brokers, hedge-fund managers – pay for the capital they use to earn a living.

Banks borrow from depositors, investors who buy CDs, and other banks. They have to pay interest for that capital. Likewise, virtually every actor in the financial-services food chain must pay for the right to use capital. Everyone, that is, except insurance companies.

Now just follow me here for a second... Insurance companies take the premiums they've collected and invest that capital in a range of financial assets.

Assume, just for the sake of argument, that they earn 10% each year on their premiums. (That is, they make 10% on their underwriting.) And assume they invest only in the S&P 500... What do you think the average return on their assets will be each year? In this hypothetical example, their return would be 10% plus whatever the S&P 500 returned.

In reality, of course, few insurance companies can make such a large underwriting return. And few insurance companies invest a large percentage of their portfolio in stocks. Most stick to fixed income to make sure they can always pay claims. But the point remains valid. By compounding underwriting profits over time, year after year, into the financial markets, insurance companies can produce very high returns.

Here's the best part: Insurance companies don't really own most of the money they're investing. They invest the "float" they hold on behalf of their policyholders.

Float is the money they've received in premiums, but haven't paid out yet. Underwritten appropriately, this is a risk-free way to leverage their investments and can result in astronomical returns on equity over time.

Just look at insurance company No. 1 in the earlier chart. Here it is again...

What Kind of Business Always Beats the Market?

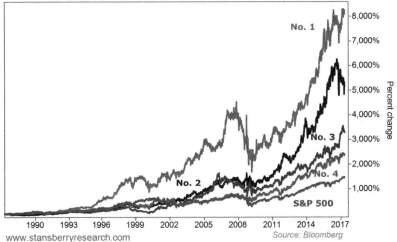

www.stansberryresearch.com   Source: Bloomberg

Company No. 1 has produced five times the S&P 500's long-term return. Can you think of any investor, anywhere, who has done anything like that? There isn't one. *That kind of performance was only possible because, using a small equity base, the firm has profitably invested underwritten float into solid investments, year after year.*

Do you like paying taxes? If you do... well, you won't like insurance stocks. They have *huge* tax advantages. Insurance is, far and away, the most tax-privileged industry in the world. *Many of their investment products are totally protected from taxes.*

And their earnings are sheltered, too. *Insurance companies don't have to pay taxes on the cash flow they receive through premiums because, on paper, they haven't technically earned any of that money.* It's not until all the possible claims on the capital have expired that the money is "earned."

So unlike most companies that have to pay taxes on revenue and profits before investing capital, insurance companies get to invest all the money first. *This is a stupendous advantage.* It's like being able to invest all the money in your paycheck – without any taxes coming out – and then paying your tax bill 10 years from now.

I realize that I can't make you (or anyone else) actually invest in insurance stocks. And I know that no matter what I say, you probably never will. It's a tough industry to understand, filled with financial concepts and tons of jargon. But there are two reasons the smartest guys in finance wind up in insurance, one way or another...

1.   It pays the best.

2.   It takes real genius to understand.

But my goal is to make it so easy to understand and follow that any reasonably diligent person can do so. I want to simply show you the one number you've got to know to invest safely and successfully.

The One Number You Need to Know to Invest Safely and Successfully

Normal measures of valuation don't apply to insurance companies. Why not? Because regular accounting considers the "float" an insurance company holds as a liability. And technically, of course, it is. Sooner or later, most (but not all) of that float will go out the door to cover claims.

But because more premiums are always coming in the door, float tends to grow over time, not shrink. So in this way, in real life, float can be an important asset – by far the most valuable thing an insurance company owns. But there's one important catch...

Float is only valuable if the company can produce an underwriting profit. If it can't, float can turn into an expensive liability.

That's why the ability to consistently underwrite at a profit is the key – the whole key – to understanding what insurance stocks to own. Outside of underwriting discipline, almost nothing differentiates insurance companies. And they have no other way to gain a competitive advantage.

Warren Buffett – who built his fortune at Berkshire Hathaway largely on the back of profitable insurance companies – explained this in his 1977 shareholder letter:

> Insurance companies offer standardized policies, which can be copied by anyone. Their only products are promises. It is not difficult to be licensed, and rates are an open book. There are no important advantages from trademarks, patents, location, corporate longevity, raw material sources, etc., and very little consumer differentiation to produce insulation from competition.

Thus, the basis of competition between insurance companies is *underwriting*. That is... **to be successful, insurance companies must develop the ability to accurately forecast and price risk**. And they must maintain their underwriting discipline even during "soft" periods in the insurance market when premiums fall.

Our team tracks nearly every major P&C insurance company in the U.S. and in Bermuda (where many operate to avoid U.S. corporate taxes completely). We rank every firm by long-term underwriting discipline. We've done the legwork for you. All you have to do is know what price to pay.

So if normal accounting doesn't apply for insurance stocks, how do you value them? Again, we went to the master, Warren Buffett, to see what he was willing to pay for well-run insurance companies.

Back in 2012, we found data on three of Buffett's biggest insurance purchases. In 1998, he bought General Re for $21 billion, which added $15.2 billion to Berkshire's float and $8 billion in additional book value. So Buffett paid $0.94 for every $1 of float and book value.

Before that, in 1995, Buffett bought 49% of GEICO for $2.3 billion, which added $3 billion to Berkshire's float and $750 million in additional book value. So Buffett paid $0.61 for every dollar of float and book value.

And way back in 1967, Buffett paid $9 million for $17 million worth of National Indemnity float. That's $0.51 for every $1 of float. Looking at these numbers, we expect to pay something between

$0.75 and $1 for every dollar of float and book value.

In short, there are two fundamental rules to investing in insurance stocks...

Rule No. 1: Make sure the company earns an underwriting profit almost every year, no exceptions.

Rule No. 2: Never pay more than 75% of book value plus float.

Most investors will never be able to make these investments because they don't understand why underwriting discipline is so critical. And they have no ability to accurately calculate float.

In my monthly newsletter *Stansberry's Investment Advisory*, we've done all the hard work for you. Our insurance value monitor looks for high-quality P&C insurers that are trading for about 50% of float-plus-book value – all of which consistently produce underwriting profits and generate realized investment returns, while growing float, book value, and the investable asset base.

– Chapter 3 –

A Sector That's Even Better Than Insurance

Pro baseball Hall of Famer Ted Williams didn't bat .406 in 1941 by swinging at every pitch.

He carefully broke down the strike zone and decided to only swing at pitches that were in his favorite spots – his own personal strike zone. He knew he had a much better chance of hitting those pitches than the pitchers had of throwing it into the few places where he wouldn't swing. *Ted Williams only struck out 27 times that season.*

As an investor, you'll be inundated with "pitches" everywhere you go – cocktail parties, the dentist office, and, of course, CNBC. Most investors swing at every hot stock tip they get.

You've got to avoid "the herd" like the plague.

Sometimes, the signs of this herd behavior are easy to see. For example, you can usually find a handful of stocks whose shares are valued for more than $10 billion and trade at more than 10 times their annual revenues.

Only a handful of businesses are created every decade that are worth this kind of valuation. And even if they're worth it, it's almost certain that, sooner or later, you'll have the opportunity to buy in at a much more reasonable price.

As an example of what usually happens to these kinds of stocks, I'd point to the social-media service Twitter (TWTR). In 2015, Twitter traded for a $19 billion in market cap and 10 times sales.

This company has serious business problems, but was hyped by promoters and caught the public's eye. If you followed the herd into Twitter then, you'd have lost 70% over the next year.

Twitter (TWTR)

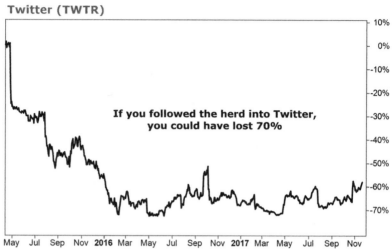

If you followed the herd into Twitter, you could have lost 70%

When you hear about companies like Twitter, it's best to just let those pitches fly by. Like Ted Williams, it's best to simply wait for an easy, fat pitch coming right through the sweet spot.

The more time I spend in the financial markets, the more convinced I become that *most* investors should only buy stocks in these few "sweet spots." In these areas, outside investors have the tools to decide whether or not a stock is *in the strike zone*.

If you can learn to limit yourself to only making capital commitments in these areas – your personal "strike zone" – I'm certain you can vastly improve your results.

In this chapter, I'm going to show you how to find outstanding long-term results in *capital-efficient* stocks. And lucky for outside passive investors, one sector of the stock market is both easy to understand and crowded with capital-efficient companies.

Simple question: Do you think you could name any of the 20 best-performing stocks in the S&P 500 in the 50 years between 1957 and 2007? Wharton economist Jeremy Siegel wanted to answer this question thoroughly.

It's not as easy to figure out as you might think because the composition of the S&P 500 changes frequently. Siegel had to go back and get the actual list of stocks from 1957 and then follow each one, carefully, to see how much they paid out in dividends, spinoffs, mergers, and liquidations.

So... what were the real best-performing stocks over that 50-year period?

TOP PERFORMERS IN S&P 500
(1957 - 2007)

Company	Annualized Return
Philip Morris	19.8%
Abbott Labs	16.5%
Bristol-Myers	16.4%
Tootsie Roll	16.1%
Pfizer	16.0%
Coca-Cola	16.0%
Merck	15.9%
PepsiCo	15.5%
Colgate-Palmolive	15.2%
Crane	15.1%
H.J. Heinz	14.8%
Wrigley	14.7%
Fortune Brands	14.6%
Kroger	14.4%
Schering-Plough	14.4%
Procter & Gamble	14.3%
Hershey Foods	14.2%
Wyeth	14.0%
Royal Dutch Pet.	13.6%
General Mills	13.6%

www.stansberryresearch.com   Source: Jeremy Siegel, The Future For Investors

Almost without exception, these companies sell high-margin products (some are *extremely* high-margin) in stable industries that are dominated by a handful of *well-known brand names*.

Look at the top 10 names on the list – the ones that produced 15%-plus annual returns. My bet is that most of you have at least three or four of these companies' products in your house at all times.

Crane, by the way, is the obvious exception. What is it that Crane (a maker of high-margin industrial parts) has in common with these other companies? It's extraordinarily *capital-efficient*.

Because of Crane's excellent, storied reputation (it has been in business since 1855), the unique, proprietary nature of its products, and the stable, long-term nature of its business, Crane doesn't have to spend a fortune on brand advertising or building new manufacturing plants to come up with new products every few years.

This means that as sales grow, the amount of capital that must be reinvested in the business doesn't grow much – or at all. Over the last 10 years, Crane has earned gross profits of about $8.5 billion and spent just $346 million on capital investments.

I learned the basic concepts behind capital efficiency by carefully studying the few large investments Warren Buffett made in the 1970s and 1980s. If you read his 1983 letter to shareholders, he basically gives away the whole strategy. But it's hidden... at the end of the letter... underneath the title: "*Goodwill and its Amortization: The Rules and the Realities.*"

You can read Buffett's letter if you'd like... but you'll learn more from the practical application of this strategy with my December 2007 recommendation of chocolate maker Hershey (HSY).

I believe my recommendation of Hershey will likely be the best stock pick I make in my entire career. As I said when I recommended it, *"The longer you hold this stock, the more rapidly your wealth will compound and you'll never have to sell – ever."*

In my initial recommendation, I noted how capital-efficient Hershey is...

> Over the last 10 years, the company's annual capital spending has remained essentially unchanged. In 1997, the firm invested $172 million in additions to property and equipment. By the end of 2006, the annual capital budget had only increased to $198 million – a paltry 15%. Meanwhile, cash profits and dividends nearly doubled.
>
> This is the beauty of capital-efficient businesses: As sales and

profits grow, capital investments don't. Thus, the amount of money that's available to return to shareholders not only grows in nominal dollars, it also grows as a percentage of sales. In 1999, dividends paid out equaled 3.4% of sales. But by 2006, the company spent $735 million on dividends and share buybacks, an amount equal to 14.8% of sales.

More than nine years later in early 2017, Hershey's sales have grown to almost $7.5 billion, but capital investments remain incredibly small – less than 5% of sales. In 2015, with gross profits of $3.4 billion, Hershey distributed $960 million to shareholders. That's roughly 28% of gross profits and far more capital than it invested in its operations ($330 million).

That's another hallmark of capital-efficient companies: *They almost always return more capital to shareholders each year than they spend in capital investments.*

Why doesn't Hershey distribute even more? It could... Cash flows from operations were more than $1.2 billion. But companies like Hershey will wait to buy back lots of stock (or make wise acquisitions) when prices are low. How can you do the same? How do you know when is the right time to buy these stocks, which almost always trade at rich premiums to the average S&P 500 stock?

Capital Efficiency in Action

www.stansberryresearch.com

You want to buy these stocks during the rare times when they're cheap enough to safely take themselves private. Again, I explained the concept when I made by 2007 recommendation...

> Hershey's enterprise value is $11.5 billion. That's the amount of money it would require to pay off all of the company's debts and buy back all of the outstanding shares of stock at the current price.
>
> The company earns more than $1 billion before taxes, interest, and depreciation. Its earnings are very consistent, and its brand places it in the upper tier of all businesses around the world. It could easily finance a bond offering large enough to buy itself – or "go private."
>
> Thus, I think it is extremely unlikely that investors will lose money buying the stock at today's price... Given the company could easily finance the repurchase of all its stocks and bonds, I believe buying this stock is no more or less risky than buying its bonds.
>
> That is the true definition of a "no risk" stock – an analysis of its cash flow shows it could afford to buy back both all of its debts and all of its shares... These situations are extremely attractive because, while you're only taking a risk that's similar to a bondholder, you're getting ownership of all of the company's future earnings.

You know when it's safe to buy these businesses by figuring out if they could finance a debt issuance *in excess* of their enterprise value. That can be a little tricky. So use a rule of thumb...

These stocks are safe to buy (and likely to produce incredible long-term results) when you can buy them for around 10 years' worth of current cash flows from operations.

You can find businesses like these by looking in the portfolios of high-quality investors. I've noticed that billionaire investor Mario Gabelli's team at Gabelli Asset Management Company Investors (GAMCI) loves these kinds of businesses.

Likewise, of course, the exchange-traded funds focused on shareholder yield – like Meb Faber's Cambria Shareholder Yield Fund (SYLD) – will always feature a lot of these names, as companies have to be reasonably capital efficient and reasonably priced if they're going to rank in the top spots in terms of shareholder yield.

Here's another big helpful hint when it comes to this type of investing: **It's critical to avoid companies that are returning huge amounts of capital to investors simply because their businesses have become obsolete**. A company like Western Union, for example, might look good on paper... but its future cash flows are seriously in jeopardy by new technologies.

If you're going to invest using this strategy, you want to stick to the highest-quality businesses, whose products are *timeless*. I always ask myself this question: *"Are my grandkids likely to want this brand and this product?"* No brand or business in the world will last forever, but you should try to focus on the stuff that's as close to forever as possible.

Here's another valuable tip. This is one of the few, genuine secrets to investing that I've ever learned. In fact, it's a little creepy, but... **A lot of the companies that fit into our model of capital efficiency sell products that are highly addictive**.

Many of the 20 best-performing S&P 500 stocks sold habit-forming products: Phillip Morris (cigarettes), Coca-Cola and PepsiCo (sugary sodas), Hershey and Tootsie Roll (chocolate and sugar), and McDonald's (fast food).

A lot of drug companies also show up: Abbott Labs, Bristol-Myers Squibb, Merck, Wyeth, Schering-Plough, and Pfizer. People often grow very loyal to brand-name drugs they need (or think they need).

When a business produces something that people love and build habits around... it's freed from having to spend a lot of money developing new products. It can send a larger percentage of revenues to shareholders. That's the essence of a capital-efficient business.

I don't expect all (or even most) of the market's leaders from 1957 to 2007 to remain at the top of the performance charts. But what I hope you'll notice is that the characteristics of the leading companies *are the same.*

New brands come along and make small changes... and get very popular. New medicines are invented. New forms of addiction are marketed successfully. If you keep your eyes open, it's not all that hard to figure out which of these products and businesses are likely to do extremely well over the long term.

TOP PERFORMERS IN S&P 500
(1996 - 2016)

Company	Symbol	Annualized Return
Monster Beverage	MNST	44.2%
Celgene Corp.	CELG	33.4%
Apple	AAPL	27.6%
Gilead Sciences	GILD	26.3%
Biogen	BIIB	25.6%
Kansas City Southern	KSU	25.0%
Express Scripts	ESRX	24.1%
O'Reilly Automotive	ORLY	22.8%
Tractor Supply	TSCO	22.2%
Ross Stores	ROST	22.0%

www.stansberryresearch.com   Source: *Bloomberg*

Here's the list of the 10 best-performing stocks in the S&P 500 over the last 20 years (on an annualized basis)...

Four of the top five firms sell high-margin, branded drugs – as long as you agree that caffeine is a highly addictive drug. Most people don't think about Monster Beverages as a drug company, but its Monster Energy drink contains more caffeine than McDonald's regular coffee does.

From the beginning of 2006 through December 2016, Monster Beverages produced gross profits of $10.6 billion. It only spent $1 billion on capital investments.

The company doesn't pay a cash dividend. But it does look after shareholders by repurchasing stock. This lowers the share count, which means shareholders get a larger stake in the pie. From 2006 to 2016, Monster repurchased more than $2.3 billion worth of stock. Investors who bought the stock in 2006 are up more than 1,700% in about 12 years.

By comparison, the S&P 500 is up around 106% over the same period. Soda giant Coca-Cola (KO) liked Monster so much, it entered into a partnership and bought 17% of the stock in 2015.

In short, even though the company has grown significantly, it has still improved operating margins and spent more on share buybacks than the capital expenditures required to keep the business running.

Monster Beverage (MNST) vs. S&P 500

www.stansberryresearch.com

By buying capital-efficient companies at good prices, you will make money in almost any market condition. Even when you're bearish or afraid of stocks in general. And here's the best part: These secrets will also show you how to outperform in bull markets. In short, these are the most valuable ideas anyone could give you about investing in stocks...

They will help you make money even when you're dead wrong about the market as a whole or the sector you're buying.

In *Stansberry's Investment Advisory*, we've done all the hard work for you. Our capital efficiency monitor looks for great businesses trading at good prices that meet five main criteria and an enhanced set of scoring metrics.

– Chapter 4 –

How to Make Commodity Investing Risk-Free

Resources undoubtedly seem like an unusual and risky investment choice. But in this chapter, we'll discuss a slight twist that hopefully will make sense to you. **It's a way of understanding commodities that actually makes them risk-free**.

When we decided to get "long" natural gas following that commodity's bottom in the spring of 2012, we went to Texas to learn all that we could on the ground about the prospects for exporting our country's massive energy bounty.

After spending months on this project, we came back with one word: propane. You see, although it was essentially against the law to export crude oil at the time – and although it would take another five years or so before liquefied natural gas (LNG) facilities that were built then would be able to export a significant amount of methane (aka natural gas) – there were facilities and boats available to export propane.

And as the price of propane plummeted because of soaring domestic supplies, one company moved aggressively to buy up and control most of the available export capacity in the U.S. As we discovered, that company was Targa Resources (TRGP).

This was one of the greatest investment opportunities I had seen in my entire career. As we explained in the December 2012 issue of my *Investment Advisory*...

> Thanks to government tariffs, regulations, and licenses, it's almost impossible to get the huge new supplies of domestic

> energy out of the U.S. The one exception is the clean-burning, easily stored NGL family of fuels – mostly propane. And Targa controls one of the country's two propane export terminals, as well as the entire associated infrastructure necessary to supply it. Besides Cheniere, that's as close to an American export monopoly as you're going to get.

At the time of our purchase, Targa was a new company that had been created by private-equity firm Warburg Pincus. The company's primary initial assets were purchased from failed energy-trading firm Dynegy. At the time we wrote about the business, few people had ever heard of Targa, even in Texas.

We followed the energy surplus, literally down the pipes, to figure out who would be able to gain the huge profits available to companies that could acquire energy supplies at U.S. prices and sell them at foreign prices. It was Targa that owned that "bridge."

By figuring this out, we helped our subscribers earn tremendous profits.

The stock marched straight up from 2011 to 2014...

Massive Profits Exporting U.S. Energy Supplies

We first recommended the stock below $60 a share. With the drop in oil prices post-2014, Targa's share price collapsed. But our subscribers made 138% in less than two years.

Now, let's get back to how we think about investing in commodities... and how, if done correctly, commodity investments can be almost risk-free. Rather than give you a bunch of theory, I'd rather show you precisely how I put these ideas to work, starting in 2012.

I was a vehement and frequent critic of "Peak Oil." Promoters of this idea were the most intellectually dishonest people I have ever met. The true believers were worse. They were criminally stupid. There was no way we were going to run out of oil or any other hydrocarbon. Not any time in the next 100 or more years.

But such arguments did scare people. They sold a lot of books. They raised a lot of money for oil companies, even for idiots who proposed importing natural gas into the American market. (That's like setting up a business to import oil to Saudi Arabia.)

Meanwhile, while the press and the promoters were crowing about Peak Oil and starting a panic, the actual leaders of the oil business in the United States were figuring out how to combine hydraulic fracking and horizontal drilling to produce huge amounts of gas and oil from shale rock.

One of the first was Mitchell Energy, which began producing huge volumes of gas out of the Barnett Shale (north of Dallas) in the early 2000s.

Devon bought the company for $3.5 billion in 2001. Note the date. By 2001, everyone in the oil business knew very well that large increases to domestic onshore production were possible. It took a while, of course, for the industry to figure out how to optimize and economize the strategies that Mitchell pioneered. Those efforts, in fact, continue today.

But everyone should have known, as I did, that new technology, massive increases to drilling, and rapidly growing production would eventually create a glut. The risk wasn't that we would run out of hydrocarbon. The risk was that too much capital would be invested in the fields and that a glut would develop.

As early as 2006, I began to warn that a huge natural gas glut was inevitable. From the June 2006 issue of my *Investment Advisory*...

> As more rigs come online and consumers use less natural gas
> because of its high price, guess what is bound to happen? A
> glut of natural gas, with more and more natural gas in storage.
> Is that happening? Is there a glut of natural gas developing?
> Right now, there's 41% more natural gas in storage than
> average for this time of year.
>
> That's how markets work: the price of the commodity goes
> up, increased production follows, consumer behavior is
> impacted by higher prices, and, eventually, a surplus leads to
> lower prices.
>
> It's not about Peak Oil. It's simply a regular commodity
> cycle. Boom precedes bust. And when it comes to natural
> gas, unlike housing, we can't just sit on the extra capacity.
> It has to be either stored or liquidated. That's why natural
> gas prices might go lower than anyone expects, for a long
> time... Natural gas could fall even further to below $3.

Keep in mind, when I wrote that, I had no idea that the global
economy would collapse in 2008. I simply knew that there was far too
much capital being put to work in oil and gas fields... that prices were
far too high based on inventories... and that marginal producers would
continue producing for years, simply to keep cash coming in the door.

In fact, as late as 2009, I was still expecting natural gas to fall below
$3 per thousand cubic feet (MCF). At a conference that March,
I famously told global resource expert and longtime natural gas
investor Rick Rule, "If you're long natural gas, you should have your
head examined." I then bet him a case of fine Bordeaux that prices
would continue falling, to below $3. They did. (Rick, being a man of
his word, paid up.)

I want you to understand... I wasn't trying to predict the future.
I simply knew that all over the U.S., formerly marginal drilling
sites were being turned into gushers with new technology that
was becoming more and more efficient. I knew that production
was soaring. And I knew that natural gas consumption was falling
because high prices were leading power companies to burn more
coal.

Supply was soaring. Demand was falling. Inventories were bulging. And best of all, the public was fully entranced by the nonsense of Peak Oil. There was only one possible outcome: a huge glut of natural gas. This isn't rocket science. It's common sense. You can see what inevitably happened in this next chart...

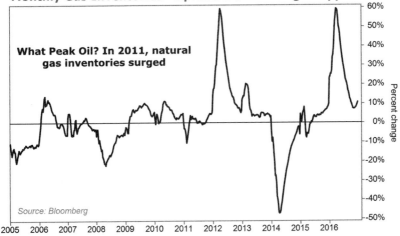

Monthly Gas Inventories - Spread from Average Supplies

Source: Bloomberg

www.stansberryresearch.com

The trick to buying commodities is to wait until there's a bust. Wait until prices for the commodity have fallen so low that producers can't produce the commodity at a profit. Wait until inventories have surged and rolled over. Wait until prices have reached a nonsensical level. And remember... these trends take a long time to develop.

With natural gas, I went from bearish to bullish in the spring of 2012. Here's what I wrote in my April 2012 issue, titled "The Best Opportunities of the Next Two Years"...

> I am extremely bullish on natural gas... For most investors, the opportunity unfolding in natural gas will be one of the best in-vestment opportunities of the next decade. Right now, natural gas is so cheap, many companies are simply flaring it off – burning it – rather than bothering to pipe it across the country and sell it. Not only that, but right now you can buy natural gas reserves in the stock market for free.

> Sooner or later, the price of natural gas will rebound sharply... and not just because it always has in the past. What will propel natural gas prices over the medium term (say, five years) is an economic truism: It's impossible for a surplus of energy to exist for long.
>
> As prices fall, more and more uses for natural gas will appear. At some price, natural gas becomes competitive with other forms of energy. You ought to buy all the natural gas you can afford because these energy resources will not be cheap forever.

By the spring of 2012, I knew a few things that gave me total confidence that natural gas prices had reached a bottom. First, I knew that at the current spot price (less than $2 per MCF), it was impossible for any of the independent natural gas companies at the time (including Devon, Chesapeake, Anadarko, and Southwestern, among others) to make money.

The next chart shows how their operating margins were collapsing as their hedges rolled off and they began transacting at the new, much lower price of gas...

Average Change in Operating Margin

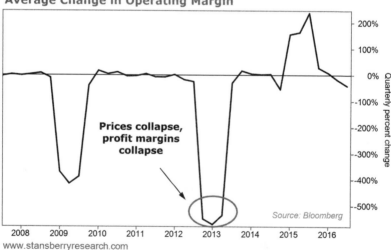

Source: Bloomberg

www.stansberryresearch.com

Next, because natural gas is only one form of hydrocarbon energy, I could see that it had reached a comparative price that was simply unthinkable. The real commodity you're buying when you buy natural gas is energy. At some price, all forms of hydrocarbons are relatively interchangeable.

That's because, compared with oil, natural gas was far too cheap on an energy-equivalent basis. For decades, oil has been about 10 times more expensive than natural gas, on average, on an energy-equivalent basis.

But by the spring of 2012, oil was trading at price equal to more than 50 times the price of natural gas. There was no way that such a price disparity would last, because one form of energy is ultimately interchangeable with another...

Oil-to-Natural-Gas Ratio

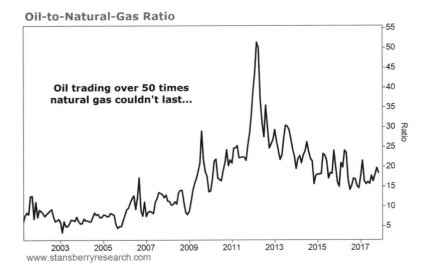

www.stansberryresearch.com

All right... by the spring of 2012, we could see that a glut had developed (as we had expected). We could see that prices had collapsed to historic lows. We could see that the marginal producers (the U.S. independents) were going to experience massive operating losses.

But how did we know the time was truly right? Our timing was dictated by significant reductions to both production and inventories.

This next chart shows the natural gas rig count maintained by oil-services giant Baker Hughes. It's the number of rigs currently working in the U.S. to produce natural gas. You can see that in 2012, the rig count plummeted. That's the producers "taking their ball and going home."

U.S. Natural Gas Rotary Rig Count

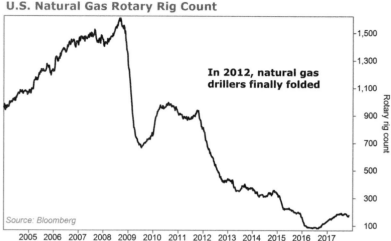

In 2012, natural gas drillers finally folded

Source: Bloomberg

www.stansberryresearch.com

This move – plus a large and surprising decline in natural gas inventories in March 2012 – was the final sign I had been waiting to see. The neat thing about commodity markets is that they are purely logical. High prices (during a boom) spur production and cause consumers to cut back consumption.

But at the bottom, the opposite occurs. Over the last few years, we saw all kinds of new demand for natural gas emerge because the price has been low. We've seen a surge in exports (see the Targa story earlier). We've seen power companies switching from coal back to natural gas. And we've seen global manufacturing relocate to the U.S. to take advantage of the surplus of cheap energy – particularly the petrochemical industry.

If you go back and look at the best-performing S&P 500 companies over the long term, you'll find that almost all the companies are either capital efficient (mostly drug companies and companies with addictive products) or energy companies. That's because the operating margins and returns on investment in the resource sector (particularly energy) can be huge.

Investing in commodity stocks is generally perceived as risky. But using a small amount of common sense and information that's widely available to all investors, it's not only possible, but it's easy to identify safe opportunities to invest in commodities. The trick is waiting until prices are so low that the entire production industry is failing and then not 'pulling the trigger' until inventories begin to sharply decline.

The other trick is remembering that these cycles are long-lived. You might only get the kind of opportunity we saw in natural gas back in 2012 once or twice every 20 years. You have to watch these markets over the long term and be prepared to make large commitments when the time is right.

The safer option than buying the producers is to focus on the "picks and shovels" companies. Take Halliburton, for example. It's the leading provider of services to the production companies I listed earlier.

The great thing about buying a well-run service company is that you get industry-wide diversification, as all production companies use Halliburton's services. Thus, you don't have to try and figure out which fields are the best or which producer is going to strike the biggest wells.

Whoever is doing best, they will be using Halliburton. You can accomplish much the same by buying ETFs that hold stakes in all of the producers, like FRAK, for example.

The point is, if you're trying to invest in the commodity price cycle, it can be very low risk if you're buying securities like service companies or ETFs that don't have any single-stock risk. If you combine this approach with buying a few of the highest-quality producers (think EOG in the Eagle Ford), I'm sure you'll be successful.

That wraps up our review of the three best sectors for outside, passive, common shareholders to invest in. Two of my three choices are intuitive: **Insurance companies can produce consistent, market-beating returns for long periods if they're able to underwrite policies at a profit.** Buying these kinds of insurance stocks is just about the safest and best form of investing I've ever discovered.

Next, **I don't think it's difficult for any investor to identify companies that have great brands, great business models (capital efficient), and products that are addictive.** I would personally avoid drug stocks, at least as individual securities, because I've found it's near impossible to figure out which company's new drug will be accepted by the FDA, etc.

That still leaves plenty of profitable businesses. Keep in mind, these are long-term bets. Real outperformance in these stocks typically won't emerge for five or 10 years. You must be patient and learn to buy at the right time (ideally, when other investors panic).

Finally, although most investors think investing in commodity businesses is very risky... I believe if you're willing to time the commodity price cycle and if you focus on "picks and shovels" plays, these investments can be among the safest you'll ever make.

In the right circumstances, you can produce trades with little downside and huge upside potential. Just remember to wait for historically low prices, collapsing profit margins (in the producers), and suddenly shrinking inventories.

– Chapter 5 –

Our Most Controversial Strategy: Beating the Market

Out of all of the things I've said or written in my career, the thing that gets me in the most "hot water" is my view that you can and should time the market.

When I write "you," I don't mean some representative sample or some investor somewhere. No, I mean you... the person reading this book... the person who is going to put his savings at risk when he invests in the stock or bond market. You.

A lot of people – even some smart ones – believe trying to time the market is a fool's errand. They argue that the best you can do is simply plow your savings, year after year, into a mutual fund or index fund. These folks make a whole range of arguments and back them up with plenty of "facts."

They'll cite academic studies and average investor results. They will say, again and again, that "no one" can beat the market, so why should anyone try?

I disagree... completely.

Let's start here. Let's say they're right. If the market is really efficient, it shouldn't matter when you invest or what you buy. If that's really the case, then why not try to do better? As long as you're investing in something, you should do alright, according to these folks. So what's the harm in trying to beat the market?

And here's another way to look at it. The efficient-market folks love to argue that it's impossible for the average investor to beat the market because it's impossible for most people to beat the average result.

At some point, it is a mathematical certainty that not everyone can beat the market. But just because something is "true" on average or across a population doesn't necessarily mean it must be true for you.

For example, I might argue on average, everyone who marries will end up with a marginally attractive spouse of normal intelligence. Therefore, you're probably wasting your time trying to find a beautiful and intelligent person to marry you. In theory, that might be good advice. But was that your dating strategy? If you had dated any dog that would have you, would you have married the spouse you wanted?

In short... when it comes to a lot of important things in our lives, getting better-than-average results is a worthy goal. Luckily for investors, I don't believe beating the market is nearly as hard as trying to date a supermodel.

I'm 100% convinced that anyone with normal intelligence and a modicum of emotional stability can do it. There are a few simple and logical reasons why...

The reasons come from Wall Street's irrational focus on short-term "earnings" and most investors' total lack of discipline. In this chapter, I'm going to give you my four steps to timing the market. **If you use my strategy, I guarantee you can double your average investment results over 10 years... or maybe even do a lot better.**

But listen... there's an entire army of people out there whose careers depend on you never doubting the idea that the markets are perfectly efficient and you can't beat the market. If you speak to any of these millions of people in the financial services industry about my ideas, they will tell you I'm a fool, liar, or fraud. So get ready for an argument. Listen carefully. You'll notice these folks won't ever discuss the merits of my actual strategy.

You see, the financial industry can only survive and prosper if you're willing to give it your assets to manage. The industry needs you to believe that it's always a good time to put your money in the market. And it needs you to believe that you can't do it yourself. That's why when I write things like this essay, folks in or supported by the financial industry go bananas.

As far as who is right and wrong... listen to what one of the wisest newsletter writers ever, the late Richard Russell, said about market timing in his classic essay, *Rich Man, Poor Man*...

> In the investment world, the wealthy investor has one major advantage over the little guy, the stock market amateur and the neophyte trader. The advantage that the wealthy investor enjoys is that he doesn't need the markets... The wealthy investor doesn't need the markets because he already has all the income he needs...
>
> The wealthy investor tends to be an expert on values. When bonds are cheap and bond yields are irresistibly high, he buys bonds. When stocks are on the bargain table and stock yields are attractive, he buys stocks.
>
> When real estate is a great value, he buys real estate. When great art or fine jewelry or gold is on the "give away" table, he buys art or diamonds or gold. In other words, the wealthy investor puts his money where the great values are.
>
> And if no outstanding values are available, the wealthy investor waits. He can afford to wait. He has money coming in daily, weekly, monthly. The wealthy investor knows what he is looking for, and he doesn't mind waiting months or even years for his next investment.
>
> But what about the little guy? This fellow always feels pressured to "make money." And in return, he's always pressuring the market to "do something" for him. But sadly, the market isn't interested.
>
> When the little guy isn't buying stocks offering 1% or 2% yields, he's off to Las Vegas or Atlantic City trying to beat the house at roulette. Or he's spending 20 bucks a week on

> lottery tickets, or he's "investing" in some crackpot scheme
> that his neighbor told him about (in strictest confidence, of
> course).
>
> And because the little guy is trying to force the market to do
> something for him, he's a guaranteed loser. The little guy
> doesn't understand values, so he constantly overpays... The
> little guy is the typical American, and he's deeply in debt.

Now... think about what Richard Russell said. Ask yourself, do you
invest like the poor man or the rich man? How much do you know
about the value of what you've bought? How long did you wait for
the right opportunity to buy it? What's your downside? What are you
expecting as your result? In a year? In three years? In five years? In
10 years?

The poor man can't even imagine a 10-year investment return.
Nothing he buys lasts that long. Of course, if you want to get rich
in stocks, almost everything you buy should last that long. It's the
compound returns that will make you rich, not the quick trades.

What does Warren Buffett, perhaps the greatest investor ever, say?
Is the market so perfectly efficient that knowledgeable and patient
investors have no opportunity to earn excess returns? Buffett argues
that all the value investors he knows – those who broadly followed
the tenets of Ben Graham and David Dodd, authors of the value-
investing bible *Security Analysis* – have beaten the market by a wide
margin.

This isn't an accident or a coin flip. These investors all used the same
principles to guide their choices. Their picks were not random or
lucky. They involved all different types of securities and strategies.
The only common theme was an intense focus on understanding the
value of each security purchased.

As Warren Buffett wrote in *The Super Investors of Graham and
Doddsville*...

> The common intellectual theme of the investors
> from Graham-and-Doddsville is this: They search for

discrepancies between the value of a business and the price of small pieces of that business in the market.

I'm convinced that there is much inefficiency in the market. These Graham-and-Doddsville investors have successfully exploited gaps between price and value.

When the price of a stock can be influenced by a "herd" on Wall Street with prices set at the margin by the most emotional person, or the greediest person, or the most depressed person, it is hard to argue that the market always prices rationally. In fact, market prices are frequently nonsensical.

I have seen no trend toward value investing in the 35 years that I've practiced it. There seems to be some perverse human characteristic that likes to make easy things difficult. The academic world, if anything, has actually backed away from the teaching of value investing over the last 30 years. It's likely to continue that way.

Ships will sail around the world but the Flat Earth Society will flourish. There will continue to be wide discrepancies between price and value in the marketplace, and those who read their Graham & Dodd will continue to prosper.

Step 1 in our guide to beating the market is based on the ideas of the men above. **Before you buy a stock or bond (or anything else), ask yourself, "What's the intrinsic value of what I'm buying? And how does that intrinsic value compare with what I'm going to have to pay for it?"** Always make sure you're buying at a good price.

There are lots of ways to estimate intrinsic value. And as with the value of a house, there isn't one right answer. If I asked you to estimate the value of your home, you could give me a range based on similar sales in your area.

You could tell me "replacement cost" based on what a lot nearby would cost and the construction costs. You could give me the tax basis. And I could look up what the insurance company estimates your house is worth. (That's usually the most accurate.)

The point is, people of normal intelligence can figure out what something is really worth. When it comes to publicly traded stocks, plenty of information is available to help you do the same.

When we look at stocks, we generally assign them an intrinsic value that's based on cash flow (how much cash this company can generate) for operating companies or a "take-out" price for asset-development stocks.

In general, public companies fall into one of these two categories. They're either operating businesses (which are designed to make annual profits) or asset-development businesses (which may have many years of losses as they build out something like a gold mine, oilfield, or new drug).

Simple rules of thumb? *Never pay more than about 10 times the maximum annual free cash flow for operating companies. Never pay more than half of the appraised value of an asset-development company.*

The next part of our strategy to "time" the market – **Step 2** – is even easier.

Learn to make big commitments only when other investors are clearly panicking, stocks are cheap, and extremely safe investments are available. This is what most people mean when they say market "timing." This is what I mean when I say "allocate to value." Two quick examples...

First, in the fall of 2008, investors were clearly panicking. Warren Buffett even wrote a letter to the *New York Times* explaining why it was time to buy stocks hand over fist – and was criticized on CNBC for doing so! If there has ever been a better contrarian indicator, I've never seen it.

Meanwhile, you could have bought shares of iconic beer maker Anheuser-Busch (BUD) – a stock I first recommended in 2006 – for around $50 for several weeks in October and November 2008. At the time, global brewer InBev had an all-cash deal in place to buy the stock for $70 per share. I told investors the situation was so safe, they should put 25% of their assets into the shares.

It was the easiest and safest way to make a lot of money I'd ever seen. Even if the deal fell through (and it couldn't; it was an all-cash deal at a reasonable price)... the stock was worth far more than $50 a share. In my view, there was zero downside and an almost certain $15-$20-per-share profit in just a few days.

A few months later – in February 2009 – shares of renowned jeweler Tiffany were trading for less than $25. The company has large inventories of gold and precious stones. Subtracting the value of its inventory from its debt load and dividing by the shares outstanding gave you liquidation value of around $24 per share.

In short, you could buy Tiffany – one of the premier luxury brands in the world – for the value of its current inventory. That means, you could have gotten the real estate, the brand, and all the future profits for free.

Again, I remember the specifics of the trade because I wrote about this situation to subscribers. It's times like these when you must be willing to make large commitments.

Fine, you might say. But what should I do, just hold cash for years or decades, waiting for a perfect situation? Stocks were only as cheap as they were in 2009 three or four times over the last 100 years.

No, I don't argue that you should stay 100% in cash until stocks crash. That is probably the biggest misunderstanding most investors have about our advice. We never advocate selling everything.

We never believe that we can predict the future accurately. Instead, we want to build a portfolio that will thrive over time, no matter what happens. At market highs, we see that stocks are no longer great values. It's harder for us to find good opportunities. And so, we've told subscribers, to begin building cash.

When you sell something, sock away the profits until better opportunities emerge. When do you sell? Well, that depends. But no matter what, follow your trailing stop losses. And that leads us to...

Step 3: Stay reasonably diversified, use trailing stop losses, and always maintain a large cash reserve. Here we part ways with most value investors. A lot of good value investors refuse to use trailing stop losses. Instead, they hope to sell when stocks become too expensive. But in our experience, it's nearly impossible for most investors to know when to sell.

Therefore, we want to focus on buying at the right time. Then we simply admit that we're not going to sell at the optimal point. We just can't predict how high stocks will go. And we want to capture as much of that upside as possible. Using trailing stops allows us to do this.

If you're not sure how to use them, please visit TradeStops.com for more information. Also, it's important to never give your stockbroker your stop-loss points. And never, ever base your stops on intraday prices. If you put your stops in the market (which is what happens when you give them to your broker)... events like a flash-crash can wipe you out.

If you remain dedicated to only buying stocks at a discount from their intrinsic value... if you become a connoisseur of value... and if you only make large investments when other investors are panicking, you should find that it's easy to keep a cash reserve.

But how many stocks should you own? What's reasonably diversified? I recommend never owning more stocks than you can completely understand and follow.

A good test is: Can you explain the stocks in your portfolio and why you bought them (the elevator pitch) to a friend without using notes or looking at your portfolio? If you can't, you don't know your investments well enough to own them or you're trying to follow too many.

You're not going to be able to find more than a handful of extraordinary investments at any given time. Why own anything that's not extraordinary?

Another good test for your portfolio is to make sure that there's not a single position that could cost you more than 5% of the value of your overall portfolio. Don't end up with so few large positions that a catastrophe in one stock wipes out all your other gains for the year.

The last part of our strategy (Step 4) to always beating the market is do everything you can to avoid the damage from fees and taxes to maximize your long-term, compound returns.

Whenever possible, keep your assets in vehicles that allow you to compound your investments tax-free. Minimize trading and fees, which enrich your broker, not you. Look for companies whose management is well-known for doing tax-efficient deals and rewarding shareholders in tax-efficient ways. And always reinvest your dividends – either in the same companies or in new ones that offer better value.

Studies show that most investors perform terribly when managing their own assets. That doesn't mean that you can't do well. It does mean that the odds are stacked against you. So read and reread this list. Start living by it.

1. Never buy a stock whose intrinsic value you can't estimate reliably – and always get a big discount when you buy.

2. Allocate to value: Wait to make major investments when other investors are panicking and truly safe, outstanding opportunities abound.

3. Use good money-management techniques. Follow position-sizing guidelines and trailing stop losses. Never own more positions than you can carefully follow. Always keep a large cash reserve.

4. Do everything you can to avoid fees and taxes. Simply avoiding a 2% annual fee against your asset base (by not using money managers) is the No. 1 surest way to outperform your peers.

– Chapter 6 –

The Funds Your Broker Should Tell You About

You don't have to settle for poorly run mutual funds or "buy everything" exchange-traded funds.

A handful of nearly secret investment funds that trade on the public market have excellent track records and treat their shareholders with great care and respect. Best of all, outside of paying a one-time brokerage fee, it *costs nothing* to own these funds.

In this chapter, I am going to detail the funds you can join and the secret "backdoor" way you can buy them.

The summary is simple: You can invest alongside the best and brightest investors in the world... You can gain substantial tax advantages (in some cases) by doing so... And executing these trades is no more difficult (or more expensive) than simply buying a stock.

Let's start there: Do you have any of your assets with renowned investors Prem Watsa or Carl Icahn? What about Sardar Biglari? He's one of the most talented young activist investors in the world. Do you think having at least some of your long-term savings with these guys would be a good idea?

I would argue that even if you're a professional investor and working on your portfolio full time, you're unlikely to produce long-term results on par with these guys. They're the best in the world, and they have the best analysts working for them – guys in their 20s and 30s who are blindingly smart and work 80 hours a week.

There are three reasons why more investors don't invest with these guys. First, obviously, most people don't know how. They think they have to have millions to get into their hedge funds. They don't know that many of the most successful investors in the world offer their portfolios to public market investors.

The next problem is harder to solve: These holding companies typically have complex structures that make them difficult to analyze and understand. I'll do what I can to show you how to make sense of them. But if you're going to invest in these firms, you have to read their annual reports and their quarterly reports.

You should go to the annual meetings, too. There's no substitute for looking these guys in the eye and hearing about their plans.

Finally... you have to be prepared for significant volatility. These guys are essentially leveraged financial firms. That means when a cold wind blows in the financial sector, these stocks are going to get "blown around."

Warren Buffett's Berkshire Hathaway saw its share price drop 50% twice during Buffett's tenure (1974 and 2000). But the intrinsic value of Berkshire Hathaway didn't change much at all.

With these kinds of companies, you must understand what you own and what it's worth. The public equity markets do a terrible job at pricing these kinds of companies.

Let's start with the most famous – Carl Icahn. One public vehicle owns essentially all of Icahn's investment assets – Icahn Enterprises (Nasdaq: IEP). The company owns his direct investments, including automotive, railcar, casinos, energy, metals, mining, food packaging, home fashion, and real estate.

Carl Icahn personally owns 90% of the stock, which has a market capitalization of $7 billion and holds around $13 billion in debt.

In 2016, the stock traded at a significant premium to book value. A good time for you to get in is when it's trading at book value or less.

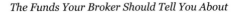

Icahn Enterprises (IEP)

Share price

Valuation

Source: Bloomberg

2008 2009 2010 2011 2012 2013 2014 2015 2016 2017
www.stansberryresearch.com

The next investor we'll discuss is on his way to becoming a financial titan. It may well pay huge dividends to hop on the boat before he's as big as someone like Icahn.

His name is Sardar Biglari. His company is Biglari Holdings (NYSE: BH).

Like Buffett, Biglari holds an annual meeting worth attending every year that features a tough Q&A session that lasts for hours. He, like Buffett, also writes annual letters that are brilliant. But unlike Buffett, he's known for being arrogant and doesn't suffer fools gladly... at all. Naturally, I like him.

Whatever you think of his personality, his track record is among the best in the world. He used a private investment fund to take over and turn around fast-food chain Steak 'n Shake, a move that required tremendous financial risk-taking and true operational excellence.

Biglari is one of the few executives who can operate at a high level both on the financial side and on the business side – something that Sears Holdings CEO Eddie Lampert, for example, has failed to do.

Out of all the young guys in finance these days, Biglari is the most fascinating... and I believe he will become the most successful.

Biglari Holdings is still small – the market cap is less than $1 billion. From 2011 to 2016, Biglari grew the firm's book value an average 13% annually. The insurance operations should grow this figure substantially.

Biglari Holdings (BH)

Source: Bloomberg

www.stansberryresearch.com

The last "secret" fund I'd like to show you isn't a secret at all. It's a well- known insurance company – Fairfax Financial – headquartered in Toronto. What makes Fairfax unusual is that like Buffett's Berkshire Hathaway, the company invests most of its insurance float in value stocks. Its chief investment officer – Prem Watsa – is one of the world's leading value investors.

Over the last 30 years, Fairfax Financial has grown its book value an average of 20% annually. We added it to our *Stansberry's Investment Advisory* model portfolio in January 2017. By November 2017, Fairfax Financial traded at a slight premium to book value.

You can find it under the Canadian ticker symbol FFH. The stock also trades on the U.S over-the-counter (OTC) market with ticker symbol FRFHF.

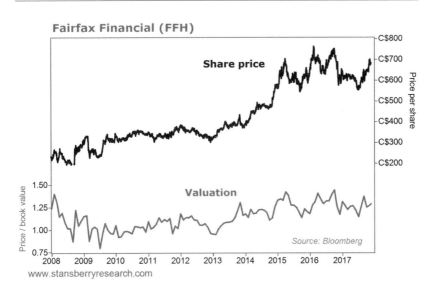

Fairfax Financial (FFH)

Share price

Valuation

Source: Bloomberg

www.stansberryresearch.com

What Should I Do With This Information?

First, read whatever you can from these companies' public filings. Fairfax Financial, for example, reports its positions in a "13F" report to the SEC each quarter, giving you a free look at what one of the world's best value investors is buying.

I recommend buying shares of these firms when they're selling for book value or less. They will grow their book value at a faster rate than you will grow your overall portfolio. Nothing is certain, of course... but the odds favor these investors in a massive way.

Here's a tip: From time to time, these shares trade for less than book value. That's because most investors don't understand insurance stocks or because, in Biglari's case, most investors simply think he's going to fail in his efforts to turn around or take over new businesses.

What you should do is wait, read, meet, and learn. By that, I mean watch the stocks carefully. Read their quarterly and annual reports. Attend their annual meetings. (Buy one share so you can attend.) Learn what makes these businesses work.

And when you feel comfortable that you really understand what they do and why, begin to invest. **Do your best to buy when other**

investors won't. And try to pay less than book value.

You might also wait to see when these financial gurus – Icahn, Biglari, and Watsa – begin to buy their shares. If you're patient, you'll get those opportunities.

Here's another tip. During periods of market uncertainty, these stocks will fall – usually more than the market falls. That means the prices on options for these stocks will tend to be rich. **That makes these stocks great vehicles on which to sell put options.**

You can sometimes garner huge premiums, which can greatly reduce your acquisition cost. This strategy can reduce the cost of buying stocks like these by 25%-50% over the course of a year.

– Chapter 7 –

A Four-Step Test for Great Investments

In this chapter, we're going to do something that's hard for most people. It involves some math. It involves thinking hard about rather abstract ideas. It will likely involve learning new jargon, which is probably the hardest part.

This is something most people will go to great lengths to avoid. So let me tell you why you should first calculate these four things every time you buy another stock...

This four-part test is a nearly foolproof way to evaluate the quality and the value of *any* business. It will allow you to quantify, with surprising precision, exactly what makes a given business great, average, or poor.

This knowledge will allow you to make vastly better and more informed decisions about what any business is worth and what you should be willing to pay for it on a per-share basis. But that's not the best reason to learn this four-part test.

The real secret is, once you develop the discipline to *always* do this work before you buy any stock, you'll never make a quick decision to buy a stock ever again. Once you add something that's hard to do, that requires a little bit of time, a little rigor, and a little discipline to your investment process, you're going to greatly reduce the number of stocks you buy.

You're also going to radically improve the quality of the stocks you're willing to invest in because you'll have the skills to do so. And that will eliminate more than 90% of your investment mistakes. Remember... you don't need to find a great investment every month or even every year. You just need to find one every now and then... and have capital ready to put to work.

I believe *the No. 1 thing you need to know to be successful as an investor in common stocks is what type of business makes for a great investment*. Investment legend Warren Buffett says the same thing. He puts it this way...

> Your goal as an investor should simply be to purchase, at a rational price, a part interest in an easily-understandable business whose earnings are virtually certain to be materially higher five, 10, and 20 years from now.

So... what makes a great business? How can you be certain its earnings will materially grow over reasonable periods of time? To figure it out, let's take one of Buffett's most famous investments – Coca-Cola (NYSE: KO).

Coke sells addictive (caffeine-laced) sugar water for more than the price of gasoline all around the world. It has integrated its brand into people's lives through decades of advertising spending – an investment that has paid off tremendously. Coke has one of the world's most universally recognized and admired brands.

But how do these advantages translate into hard numbers? The most obvious characteristic of a great business is **high profit margins**. High margins are proof of a great brand, a superior product, or some form of regulatory capture that permits greater-than-normal profitability. On every dollar of revenue in 2016, *Coke earned nearly $0.21 in cash*. And it brought in $42 billion in revenue.

To figure out exactly how much money Coke earns in cash, we simply look at the company's Statement of Cash Flows, under the line: "total cash flow from operating activities." We see that in 2016, this was $8.8 billion.

(The "Statement of Cash Flows" is one of four financial statements published in every SEC form 10-K, along with the Income Statement, Balance Sheet, and Statement of Comprehensive Income. You can access these statements by looking at a com-any's annual report, which is available on the "Investor Relations" section of its website, or by using Yahoo Finance or any number of other online databases, like Bloomberg.)

Next, we divide those cash profits by the company's total revenues ($42 billion), which you can find on the income statement. Doing the math gives you a fraction that is commonly expressed in percentage form: 21%. Coke's cash operating profit margin is 21%. It's earning $0.21 in profit on every $1 it generates in sales.

In our experience, businesses with cash operating margins in excess of 20% are world-class. If you were putting together a checklist, you could start there. **A great business must have cash operating margins greater than 20%**.

The next "mile marker" you're looking for is **capital efficiency**, which we've covered extensively. This is another concept that, like profitability, is easy for most people to grasp. All you're trying to understand with this test is *how much capital the company requires to maintain its facilities and grow its revenues*. For example, oil and gas companies are notorious for spending every penny they make on drilling more holes and building more facilities. Their capital-spending programs leave little of their profits to be distributed to shareholders (often less than zero).

One simple way to assess a company's capital efficiency is figure out whether the company in question distributes more capital back to shareholders... or spends more money "on itself" via capital-spending programs.

A great business distributes more profits to its shareholders than it consumes via capital investments. Coke, for example, spent $2.3 billion on capital investments in its own business in 2016. It spent $6 billion on dividends and $2.2 billion on net share buybacks in the same period. You can see that Coke spends far more on its shareholders than it spends on itself. (By the way, all these numbers are labeled clearly on the cash flow statement.)

What's powerful for investors about businesses like these is that you don't need lower interest rates or a raging bull market to be successful. As these businesses grow, they increase their payout amounts, year after year. It's the compounding effect of this growth that will make you wealthy. That's why Buffett says you should never buy a stock you wouldn't be happy to hold for a decade, even if the stock market was closed.

The third part of our four-part litmus test for great businesses is "**return on invested capital**." (Here comes the jargon.) Yes, it's a mouthful. But I promise, with just a little practice, you'll be able to easily calculate this figure in your head. We use this metric because there's no purer way of determining the value and the power of a company's "moat" – the degree to which the company is sheltered from profit-eliminating competition.

The business school formula for determining the precise amount of invested capital is complex and requires several different numbers (and judgments about each of them). It's a pain. And there's a much easier way to get a ballpark figure – *just add the total amount of a company's long-term debt and the total value of the company's equity capital.* You'll find both numbers as simple line items on the balance sheet.

Coke has $23 billion worth of equity capital and $47 billion worth of debt (adding the short-term debt to long-term debt). So in our book, the company has invested capital of $70 billion. On this capital in 2016, the company reported $6.5 billion worth of net income, or "earnings." Its return on invested capital is 9.36%.

A great business will have returns on invested capital of at least 20%.

You'll find Coke's net income on the aforementioned income statement. Once you have the numbers, you just do the basic math (6.5 divided by 70) to derive another percentage – 9.3%. As you'll see, this is where Coke falls a bit flat. The beverage market is ultra-competitive and Coke's brand only provides a small measure of protection against competitive pricing.

The last part of our great business test is also a bit "wonky" and will make you sound like a finance geek. It's called **return on net**

tangible assets. This number gives you the best overall measure of the quality of any business. It's similar to the more commonly used ROE ("return on equity") with two important differences.

First, measuring returns against net tangible assets takes goodwill out of the calculation. So companies with large amounts of goodwill (like companies with great brands) typically show a much higher return. Second, this measure of quality rewards companies that can borrow most of the capital they need because their results aren't cyclical.

Calculating this number is also easy. Yahoo Finance lists "net tangible assets" among its balance sheet statistics. Alternatively, you can use the company's balance sheet to calculate the number yourself.

Simply subtract Total Liabilities, Goodwill, Trademarks, and Other "Intangible" Assets from Total Assets. Then compare this number with the company's net income for the last year. In Coke's case, net tangible assets total only $1.9 billion. Coke earned a profit equal to 342% of its net tangible assets.

A great business will have a return on net tangible assets of more than 20% annually. So Coke's 342% return is a truly outstanding figure.

(Note: In some cases, a company will have more liabilities than it has tangible assets. In those cases, the math you see above no longer works because you can't divide using a negative net tangible assets figure. When that happens, we'll subtract out only *the long-term portion of total liabilities*. This provides a more meaningful number, while still measuring the company's ability to safely replace equity with debt in its capital structure.)

Putting It All Together

Putting all these factors together, our test of business greatness starts with profits. How much money, in cash, does a business earn from its operations, expressed as a percentage of its sales? The higher the margins, the better. This tells us that the company owns high-quality brands and products, as well as market position. We expect great businesses to produce cash operating margins of at least 20%.

Our second test is capital efficiency. Does the business produce substantial amounts of excess capital, and does management treat shareholders well? We test this by seeing whether shareholders receive at least as much capital each year as the business reinvests in itself. We expect a great business to distribute more profits to its shareholders than it consumes via capital investments.

The third test is return on invested capital, which is the best measure of a company's moat. Here again, we would expect to see returns on invested capital of at least 20% for it to qualify as a great business.

Finally, our last measure of great companies – return on net tangible assets – combines brand value, capital efficiency, the quality of earnings, etc. We expect returns on net tangible assets to exceed 20% annually.

Business quality is extremely important, but the stock price is equally important for investment outcomes. Our best advice is to value high-quality businesses by the amount of cash they earn before interest, taxes, depreciation, and amortization. In finance jargon, this measure of profits is called "EBITDA."

You can't use this measure with lower-quality businesses, but it works well for high-quality businesses because it allows you to quickly judge companies in different industries against each other.

Now, let me show you a trick that will show you *when* to buy a high-quality company: *We try to avoid paying more than 10 years' worth of EBITDA per share when we buy a business.*

We measure the cash earnings against the enterprise value of the business (the value of all the shares and all the debt, minus the cash in the business). But you don't need to do all this work yourself. You can find this multiple on Yahoo Finance on the key statistics page for any given stock.

Valuing businesses is a lot more difficult than evaluating their performance. You should be willing to pay more for a high-quality business that's growing.

So the Four-Step Test of Greatness is...

1. Cash operating profit margin: cash from operations / revenue (should be greater than 20%).

2. Shareholder payout ratio: capital returned to shareholders / capital expenditures (should be greater than 1).

3. Return on invested capital: net income / long-term debt + shareholder equity (should be greater than 20%).

4. Returns on net tangible assets: net income / net tangible assets (should be greater than 20%).

Bonus Step:

1. Share price multiple: enterprise value / EBITDA (ideally less than 10).

– Chapter 8 –

How to Find the Best Conditions in the World for Investors

Do you think the macroeconomic conditions in the United States are optimal for equity investors?

I don't. Optimal conditions for equity investors last existed in the U.S. in the late 1970s and early 1980s. At one point during that period, real interest rates reached as high as 10% a year in the U.S. and Treasury bonds were offering investors nominal yields as high as 15%.

With fixed income offering such large returns, equity valuations collapsed. At one point in the early 1980s, you could have bought oil major Exxon for less than five times earnings and gotten a dividend yield of nearly 8%.

We have almost the opposite conditions in 2017. Real interest rates in parts of Europe and Japan are negative. So much excess capital is in these bond markets that the sovereign borrowers no longer need to offer any effective rate of return. Central banks have flooded these markets with capital.

These conditions are terrible for equity investors, as valuations can become untethered from earnings. Stocks become expensive. And make no mistake...

U.S. stocks are expensive in late 2017. So part of my advice has been to wait until the general conditions are more favorable to long-term investors. Only make large commitments when other investors are panicking.

On the other hand... why wait? You can find developed equity markets all around the world in countries where property and contract laws are enforced and Western accounting is common. Isn't it possible that optimal conditions for equity investors exist somewhere?

Everyone has the ability today to invest in markets all over the world. Country-specific exchange-traded funds (ETFs) offer cheap and easy access to most developed markets in the world. And you can invest in some high-quality foreign companies that list their shares on the New York Stock Exchange.

Also, no law prohibits you from buying shares on foreign exchanges... And obviously, sometimes foreign markets are far more attractive than ours.

Since 2000, the number of Americans holding a valid passport has doubled. Today, more than 110 million Americans hold a passport – roughly 30% of the population.

Sadly, that doesn't mean most Americans have any real appreciation for foreign countries or cultures. It only means that post-9/11 Americans were forced to carry a passport to cross the borders with Canada and Mexico. I'm sure that far less than 30% of U.S. investors consider buying foreign stocks or investing in foreign stock market ETFs.

That doesn't make any sense to me. Some readers will think it's risky to invest outside of the U.S., where our laws and courts might not be able to protect investors. To me, that kind of thinking is laughable. It pretends that there's something particularly noble or efficacious about our legal system. If you believe that, you've never been involved with it.

Meanwhile, the facts are almost the opposite of what most Americans believe. It's far riskier to hold all your investments in one country and one currency. That's especially true when conditions are as poor as they are today for equity investors in America.

Like it or not, America is shrinking in terms of the global economy. When I was born (1972), the U.S. made up about 70% of the world's economy. By the time my sons have children, the U.S. economy will only represent about 20% of global GDP.

Many countries around the world are growing faster than the U.S. Many countries around the world have much larger potential markets. These places will offer excellent investment opportunities, ones that will often be better and safer than buying U.S. stocks.

Giving up these opportunities automatically by never considering them is like trying to win a wrestling match with one arm. You might win. But even if you do, it would have been a hell of a lot easier with both arms.

In *Stansberry's Investment Advisory*, we monitor more than 150 of the highest-quality businesses from around the world – businesses we call the "global elite."

As we've shown already in this book, the global elite always have some unique traits or qualities.

They nearly always have some competitive advantage in the market. It could be their brand, their distribution network, or a combination of several factors.

Brand value is subjective... but consider brands like Apple, Google, or Coca-Cola.

Coke's red and white logo is among the most recognized brands in the world. *Forbes* ranks Coke's brand at No. 4 in the world behind Apple, Google, and Microsoft. Facebook is ranked No. 5. Amazon is ranked No. 12.

These elite businesses usually dominate their markets. They are often the largest in the sector. Amazon became the world's largest online retailer because it knew how to serve customers with a vast range of products delivered to their homes better than its competitors. It has huge buying power, which enables it to sell stuff cheap. That makes it tough for smaller firms to compete.

Chocolate manufacturers Hershey and Nestlé are global elite businesses. Everyone knows these world-famous brands. Budweiser and Heineken are global elite beer brands.

While brand recognition often relates to consumer goods, the Global Elite Monitor contains industrial, financial, energy, and tech companies, too.

For example, Germany's business software company SAP has established itself with powerful enterprise application software.

Measuring a company's unique competitive advantage... what we call "moat"... is sometimes difficult but critical to identifying a truly elite business.

When looking at the more quantifiable traits in the business, we look for financial stability and overall performance. Sales and earnings growth, healthy gross and operating margins, balance sheet strength, and debt serviceability are among our key metrics. And we want companies that look after shareholders. Not all companies pay dividends or buy back shares. That's OK if management is reinvesting for growth. But we will apply our own valuation metric to how management allocates capital.

We also like to look at as much historical data as possible, going back 10 years or more. This allows us to see how companies have fared in bull and bear markets and watch cyclical trends. We only want to buy when we get stocks at cheap valuations.

Analyzing historical data for these companies is critical to our success as investors.

For the most part, we focus on the U.S., European, Japanese, and Chinese markets. Combined, they make up almost 70% of global GDP, and they have the most important capital markets in the world.

In *Investment Advisory*, we look for high-performing, low-volatility stocks. Most of these will be conservative companies. They'll likely have huge brands or some other unique trait that gives them a huge competitive advantage over their competitors.

– Chapter 9 –

The Advanced Course: The Only Way I Like to Trade Options

Fair warning. The secret I'm about to tell you is dangerous.

I'm going to show you how (and when) to make an absolute killing in the markets – profits that are unreasonable. I'm going to show you how I use options.

And if you use these ideas in the right way, you can produce hundreds-of-percent profits routinely and safely. But if you're careless, lazy, or greedy with these ideas... they will destroy your savings.

Let me start with some important parameters...

You should only use these techniques I'm going to show you on high-quality companies (companies with great brands, great assets, or both). And you should only use these ideas when you are 100% certain the value of the company far exceeds its current quoted price.

If you couldn't testify before Congress – with enough supporting evidence that a fair price for the business is at least 50% more than the quoted price, don't even think about using these techniques.

Likewise, **never... ever... put more than 10% of your capital at risk in any of these trades**. You can make a lot of money with these ideas, but they will produce volatile results. You cannot handle this kind of volatility unless you're using the proper position sizes. **Don't have enough capital? Don't do the trade**.

(Please... read the previous paragraph again before you continue – especially the last sentence. If you can't accurately value the business, if you aren't certain of what it's worth, or if you don't have enough capital to maintain the position at less than 10% of your portfolio, don't do the trade.)

My strategies involve using options. That statement ends the conversation for most of my readers. And that's really fine. You can be successful as an investor if you never, ever trade an option. On the other hand, if you want to make really large gains, you must use options. The key to success is never to pay for them. There's nothing wrong with taking a speculative position – like a call option – if you don't pay for it.

Let me show you exactly what I mean, using a real recommendation that we published in my *Stansberry Alpha* service. This isn't a sales presentation. I simply want to show you what I believe is the right way to use options – to use them in a way that greatly reduces your risk, greatly enhances your leverage, and can provide enormous returns on the capital you invest into the trade.

To start... you must find a security that features world-class assets and is deeply undervalued. Even as late as the end of 2012, that wasn't hard to do in the U.S. market.

For example, we'd been following the shares of MGM since mid-2008. The company, as we discussed earlier, owns most of the major hotels on the Las Vegas strip. In the mid-2000s, it decided to build the most expensive, privately financed residential development in the history of the United States the $9 billion City Center.

The project increased the number of MGM-owned hotel rooms in Las Vegas by about 50%. Some were even concerned that the Las Vegas airport didn't have the capacity to bring in enough people to fill these hotels and condos.

It was far too much new capacity at exactly the wrong time. We thought it was possible the company would go bankrupt. But we also knew if the company got additional capital, the stock would soar...

That's what happened in 2009: Wealthy oil-backed investors from the Middle East bought half of City Center. Then, during the years that followed, MGM restructured its debts, lowered interest costs, and made bankruptcy unlikely.

At that point, we needed to see one last sign before investing – a rebound in hotel rates, occupancy, and sustained revenue growth.

By 2012, MGM revenue hit a new all-time high and the company's assets were valued on the books at $27 billion. Meanwhile, the company had a market capitalization of only $10 billion. You could argue that the company was worth three times more than its stock price. Prior to the crisis, MGM had a market capitalization of $25 billion.

We recommended the stock in the July 2012 issue of my *Investment Advisory*. It was one of the best investment opportunities I had seen in my career. It was the kind of opportunity that can result in big gains in a short amount of time.

With the company's balance sheet back on solid footing, I didn't believe there was any material risk in owning the stock. So... how could we turn this good of an opportunity into a killing?

In the December 2012 *Stansberry Alpha* (our second issue), we recommended selling a put option on the stock with a strike price of $10 that expired in January 2014. A put option is nothing more than a promise to buy 100 shares of stock at a fixed price ($10, in this case) for a certain period of time (until January 2014).

The main advantage of selling a put – of merely promising to buy the stock instead of actually buying it – is leverage. To allow you to sell this option, brokers ask for a deposit that assures you can meet your potential obligation. (The amount of leverage you can get depends on your broker, but the legal minimum is only 20%.)

With a strike price of $10, investors only had to put up $2 per share. And this is hard to believe, but it's true... other investors were willing to pay us $1.36 in exchange for this promise to buy the stock.

In our view, **selling a put is less risky than buying a stock**. It requires less capital (in deposit). And assuming you pick a strike price that's below the market, your effective "buy-in price" will be lower than the price of the stock at the time of your trade.

In this case, instead of buying MGM shares at $11, we were promising to buy at an effective price of $8.64. We calculate our effective "long" price by simply subtracting the fee we got in exchange for selling the put from the strike price ($10 − $1.36 = $8.64). I hope you can understand that buying a stock at $8.64 a share is less risky than buying the same stock at $11 a share. Thus, selling **puts allows us to take less risk, but in a leveraged way**.

The main problem with merely selling puts is that it's too safe. Yes, we're earning $1.36, while only putting up $2. That's an instant return of 68%. But we're only earning that return on a sliver of our capital. If the stock takes off like we expect, we're giving up a lot of potential upside. We don't have enough capital in the trade, and we don't have an unlimited upside position.

To capture more of that upside, we can spend a portion of the cash we received for selling a put (called the "premium") to purchase a call option. A call option is the opposite of a put option. It gives us the right (but not the obligation) to buy 100 shares of stock at a fixed price for a fixed period of time.

In this case, we recommended buying a $15 call on MGM that also expired in January 2014 for just $0.57. This gave us the option of opening a 100-share position in the stock at $15 a share. Of course, we'd only exercise that if the stock traded for more than $15 by January 2014.

As you can see, it costs almost nothing. And it requires zero deposit. Considering that even after buying this call option, we're still getting $0.79 in net premium for our promise to buy MGM (39.5% return on our margin requirement), I'd consider that a nearly free option.

I get that it's not actually free. But the point is, I don't believe you should ever buy an option unless you've found a way to finance it. And when I can earn an immediate return of nearly 40% on the capital I've tied up in this trade and get a call option... the call is close enough to free for me.

MGM Resorts International (MGM)

MGM bounces back from the depression of 2009

www.stansberryresearch.com

After our recommendation… MGM's stock did well. After about six months, it was up more than 50%. In June 2013, we decided to take some of our profits off the table, mostly because we grew concerned about the U.S. corporate bond market (which was crashing). In hindsight, we sold much too soon. But even so, let's look at what happened.

First, we never had to put any additional capital into this trade. The stock never traded for less than our $10 strike price. Thus, we never got a "margin call."

To close the position, we had to buy back the put we'd sold. The price of the put had fallen to $0.22, leaving us with a net premium of $0.57 per share (after you account for the cost of the call option we bought). That's a reasonable 28.5% gain in about six months.

The big gains came from the call option… We sold the call option for $1.81 per share. Keep in mind, we got this call option essentially for free. We generated all the cost ($0.57) when we sold the put. So in total, on a $2 cash investment, we earned a net premium of $0.57 and call option profit of $1.81. That's a total return of $2.38 – a 119% return our $2 cash investment in only six months.

In real dollar terms, let me show you how this might have worked in a real portfolio. Let's assume you have a $100,000 portfolio. Putting

$2,000 into this trade (on margin) would have allowed you to sell 10 put contracts on MGM at our recommended $10 strike. (Remember, each contract covers 100 shares.) That's only 2% of your entire portfolio.

But this trade is using 20% margin, which means your total potential margin requirement is $10,000. That's 10% of your portfolio. You're within our recommended risk boundaries. If your portfolio is smaller, you simply sell fewer put contracts. (With a $50,000 portfolio, for example, you would sell five contracts as a maximum position size.)

To sell the 10 contracts, you'd give your broker $2,000 in cash. He'd immediately hand back to you $1,360 in put premium, from which he'd take another $570 to purchase the $15 calls. You'd start out the trade up $790, almost $800 in the black. That offers you a considerable "margin of safety" – an instant return of 40% on the capital you've invested in the trade.

Realize, like in a real estate deal, if you are forced to meet a margin call, your return will decrease. That's why it's critical that you limit your trading only to deals where you can have a tremendous amount of certainty in the underlying value.

To close out this trade, you would have bought back the put option you sold earlier – but they only cost $0.22 per share to buy back. On 10 contracts, that totals $220. Thus, you earned a net option premium of $570 on your $2,000 investment in only six months.

That's nearly 30%. That's a great return. But it's not the real "juice."

The big gains came from the call option, which you were able to sell for $1.81 per share. On 10 contracts, that's $1,810. To find your total return, you simply add the money you made on net premium ($570) with the money you made from the call option ($1,810).

If your calculator works like mine, that's a total return of $2,380 in about six months on an investment of $2,000, or nearly 120%.

– Chapter 10 –

Why Discounted Corporate Bonds Are Even Better Than Stocks

I've worked hard to give you a summary of what I believe are the most valuable ideas, strategies, and secrets I've learned (so far) during my career in financial research.

I've saved the most valuable secret for last: **I firmly believe that corporate bonds are even better than stocks**.

That probably seems ironic coming from a guy who has spent his entire adult life researching stock investments and advising people from around the world on markets. I've recommended hundreds of different stocks. Was I lying then, or am I lying now?

No, I'm not lying. In fact, I'm telling you such a huge secret, it could easily lead you to never buy a stock again. I'm telling you this secret for the simple reason that it's what I would like you to do if our roles were reversed.

That's how I do business. And I know that if I serve my readers in this way by that exacting standard – everything else in my business will take care of itself.

So whatever you decide to do with this information, I hope you'll read carefully and think deeply about what I'm about to tell you.

Stocks can be fantastic investments. I try my best to only recommend the ones that will make you a lot of money. But the hardest part of my job is overcoming unbelievably bad management teams. If more investors really knew what happened in the offices of the CEOs of publicly traded companies, I promise... you'd never buy a stock again.

I've personally seen deal after deal executed – involving billions of dollars that had zero chance of ever creating any shareholder value. Likewise, I've seen CEOs refuse to make simple, logical, and necessary changes or divestitures that would have, in some cases, saved their companies from bankruptcy.

I was involved in a situation where I begged the management team of a great business to make a decision about its asset portfolio that was completely obvious, even to an outsider like me.

And yet, the suggestions – which were clearly in the best interest of all shareholders – were likely treated like an attack, an affront on the dignity of the management. The truth, of course, is that if the management team had any real dignity, it would be doing a much better job of managing its asset base.

The fact is, 90% of the time, CEOs do what's in their best interest – damn the torpedoes. That means trying to garner as many assets as possible, in the blind hope that something good eventually happens with one of them. And often enough, what's in their self-interest is diametrically opposed to what their shareholders deserve.

What won't you often see? Management teams giving themselves an honest appraisal. Not even Warren Buffett. He wrote publicly for many years that the test of his skill as a manager was to outperform the S&P 500 on an after-tax basis for any rolling five-year period.

For the first time in his entire career, he didn't achieve this goal. So what did he write in his 2014 letter? Going forward, he promised to beat the S&P 500 every six years.

He didn't say anything about his disastrous investment into ConocoPhillips at the top of the oil market in 2008 or his $10 billion investment – the largest of his entire career – into lackluster tech giant IBM. Instead, he made excuses about the size of his portfolio and "moved the goalposts" – something he had spent his career criticizing other CEOs for doing.

Keep in mind, Buffett could spin off any of the assets he doesn't want to manage anymore and quickly regain a growth rate that's more appropriate. But will he ever do so? Not a chance. And that's from the management team at one of America's most respected and beloved companies.

What can you do about it? Buffett recommends only buying businesses that, as he says, "could be run by monkeys." After all, he warns investors, "sooner or later, that's what will happen." Too bad nobody realized he was making a prediction about Berkshire.

Is that a cheap shot? I don't know. Probably. But it's amazing how every management team – even Buffett – can devise wondrous excuses for miserable performance. What can you do about it? Well, that's easy: Don't give them any cheap capital. They don't deserve it.

"All right, tough guy," you're probably saying. *"If we're not going to put our money into stocks, what should we do? We can't trade commodities... We'll get killed. We can't hold cash... The Fed is printing the dollar into oblivion. Fixed income? You must be kidding – how can anyone survive on earning less than 6% a year?"*

Yes, **the answer is fixed income**. And you won't be surprised to learn that it's a kind of fixed income that your broker probably won't sell you... at least, not easily.

It's a kind of fixed income that offers you incredibly high rates of income – more than 10% – and huge capital gains, too... capital gains that can rival (or even exceed) the largest gains you've ever made in stocks.

But before I get into the details of how to make this work for you, I want to pause for a moment and talk about why this works.

American managers act like capital is free. They make terrible capital-allocation decisions. Far from "allocating to value," they constantly allocate to popularity. As a result, they chronically overpay for super-low-quality assets. The way you can make this work for you is simple: You lend them the money.

Capital isn't free, of course. And if you take a more senior position in the capital structure (bonds versus stocks), you can make sure that you nearly always get paid. The management team doesn't have the option of whether to reward you for your investment or not. It must pay the coupon on your bond or else the company will go bankrupt, its assets will be sold, and its employees will be out of a job.

I would bet that more than 90% of my subscribers have never purchased an individual corporate bond. That's madness. If I could, I wouldn't let any of my customers buy stocks until they had invested in corporate bonds.

Bonds are far safer than stocks. The average recovery rate on corporate bonds in default is around $0.45 on the dollar, according to financial services firm Standard and Poor's.

No, you don't want to try to buy a bond of a company headed for bankruptcy. Of course not. Recovery in bankruptcy is always uncertain and there are no guarantees, especially not these days, when the government and the courts are doing crazy things.

But it's an indication that, for most bonds, at the very worst, you're going to get back a good portion of your money. That's especially true if you follow my advice, which is to never pay more than $0.70 on the dollar for corporate bonds. But... I'm getting ahead of myself.

There are really three things you have to know about buying corporate bonds the right way. The right way means:

- You're going to get more than 10% a year in yield.

- You can't lose more than 35% of your investment, no matter what.

There's an overwhelming likelihood that you'll make at least a 100% total return over three years.

That's three times more than you'll make in stocks on average. The reality is, most individual investors make almost nothing (less than 3% annually) in stocks because they always sell at the worst possible time.

I say that based on studies like those done on mutual funds (by research firm Dalbar) and by a big study conducted on actual brokerage account results (by investment manager Blackrock).

Judging by our feedback e-mail and conversations I've had over many years with both investors and brokers, the same facts apply to most (not all) of my subscribers. My advice? At the very least, **make bonds the center of your portfolio going forward**.

When you own bonds instead of stocks, there are three layers that protect you from making bad decisions. **First, you don't have to worry about bonds going to zero (90% of the time)**. You are legally entitled to your coupon payments and to your share of the company's assets if it can't pay you in full.

Second, if you learn to buy at the right time (when the bond market is in distress), you will receive large amounts of income. This makes it hard to lose money overall. Like the "rich man" in the famous Richard Russell essay, having a rich stream of income makes you patient and allows for you to wait until the perfect deal comes along.

And third, bond investments normally take several years to mature. This encourages you to avoid overtrading and, again, to wait until exceptional deals appear.

But rather than blather on more about theory... I'd like to show you a real example. We'll use MGM yet again, because it's a company almost everyone understands. The Las Vegas Strip-dominating hotel and casino company is one of our favorite trophy asset businesses.

If you take a look at the company's five-year share-price history, you'll discover that MGM's shares got clobbered during the 2008-2009 financial meltdown. The shares have since rebounded about 300% from their average price during 2009 (around $10).

I discussed why this happened earlier: The company built out a massive expansion (City Center) at exactly the wrong time. But it still had great assets it could easily sell, and it didn't have too much debt.

In the middle of the crisis in 2009, the company sold one of its lowest-quality hotels (Treasure Island) for $14,000 per hotel room. Assuming it only got the same value for its more upscale hotels, the company's Vegas assets alone were worth far more than all its debts. And that assumes fire-sale pricing and ignores the company's substantial assets outside Vegas and in China.

MGM was suffering a liquidity crisis, not a solvency crisis. And that meant buying its debt was safe. You couldn't say the same thing about its stock. Investors had no idea if management would get new funding if it would be able to keep the "wolf" at bay.

Before buying its shares, you needed to wait until you could see sustained improvements in its revenues and cash flows. That's what we did.

On the other hand, buying its debt was always safe. Because no matter what stupid thing management did next, the hotels and casinos were still going to be there... And they were extremely valuable, as the sale of Treasure Island proved.

By early 2009, MGM bonds were trading for less than $0.50 on the dollar. They hit bottom at $0.30 on the dollar. Of course, nobody can know when markets will bottom and what the best available price will be.

And we won't pretend that looking back we could have gotten the "low tick" in MGM's bonds.

But any price below $0.50 on the dollar would have qualified as a world-class opportunity. At that price, the yield on the bonds would have been 15% annually. That's like Santa Claus showing up at your office with a big sack of free money. Or as I like to say about really obvious investments: horse, meet water.

Only three years later, these bonds were trading back at "par" – 100 cents on the dollar. **Over three years, these fully collateralized bonds would have doubled your money**. And you also would have collected another 45% in coupon payments.

Earning 145% in three years – without taking any substantial financial risk is a far better deal than buying any stock...

MGM Resorts International (MGM)

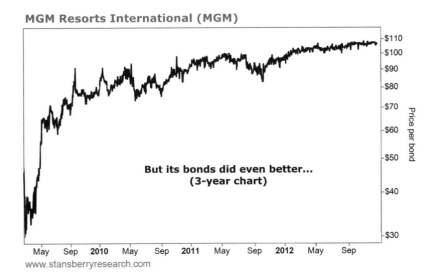

But its bonds did even better...
(3-year chart)

www.stansberryresearch.com

Sure, MGM's stockholders have done well, too. The stock is up about 240% over five years. But who knew back then if management could right the ship? Who knew what stupid thing it would do next? Who knew how long it would take?

That's the beauty of these deals... As bondholders, we truly didn't care what management did or didn't do. It was up to them to pay us or lose everything. It's like the movie *Goodfellas*. When the mob lends you money, you have to pay it back.

Recall the scene in *Goodfellas* where the mobsters burned down the poor guy's restaurant? Oh, business is bad? Too bad, pay us. Oh, a bunch of jerks ran up big tabs and won't pay them? Too bad, pay us. Oh, someone burned down your restaurant? Too bad, pay us.

Bondholders have the same exact view. Oh, global financial crisis hurt your business? Too bad, pay us.

If those big returns available in stocks are too irresistible, there's nothing stopping you from combining equity and debt into a single position. If you're fairly confident that management can bail out the ship, you can simply buy shares with the discounted portion of the bond.

Corporate bonds typically trade in face values of $1,000. So if you bought MGM's bonds at $0.50 on the dollar, you would have had $500 or so to buy shares. At the time, the stock was trading for less than $10. To make the math easy, let's say you got shares at $10. So you have a bond with a $1,000 face value (purchased at $500) and 50 shares of stock for a total investment of $1,000.

Here's the best part: No matter what happens to the shares, you should get all of your capital back because those bonds matured in 2016 and then the company had to pay you back your $1,000.

Even though the stock was really risky back then, you were protected. By late 2016, the bond would have paid you $375 in coupons... and traded at a premium to face value. And the shares would have been worth roughly $27 each, or $1,350, for a total return of 172% over five years – far more than 30% a year. And again, you really didn't take any risk in this trade.

There are, of course, plenty of pitfalls and problems associated with investing in corporate bonds. The biggest problem is that high-quality assets like MGM's aren't often available as collateral on bonds yielding more than 10%, let alone 15%. There is, however, a regular cycle in the corporate-bond market...

Once every seven to 10 years, the market completely blows up. When bond liquidations start, even the highest-quality issuers will see their bonds trading at big discounts to par. A few rules of thumb can help you easily time these cycles.

First and foremost, you want to watch the spread between high-yield corporate bonds and U.S. Treasurys. This will generally tell you whether corporate bonds are distressed or trading in the clouds.

As you can see in the next chart, the spread between high-yield bonds and U.S. Treasury bonds has rarely been this small.

When capital is this cheap and easy, you simply must stand aside from this market, as far too many loans are going to be made to far too many low-quality companies. The result will be a huge wave of debt defaults at some point between now and 2019. We can't know when it will happen – but we know it will happen. Just look back at history...

The 'Spread'

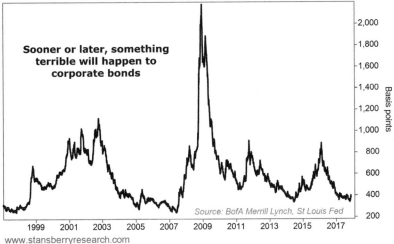

Sooner or later, something terrible will happen to corporate bonds

Source: BofA Merrill Lynch, St Louis Fed

www.stansberryresearch.com

This chart, from the U.S. Federal Reserve, shows the spread (the difference) between so-called "risk-free" bonds (based on U.S. Treasury bonds with a similar duration) and the Merrill Lynch high-yield corporate-bond index. This is the standard measure of corporate credit conditions.

When the spread is low, credit is widely available and cheap. When the spread is high, credit is tight and can be incredibly expensive. Investors should wait to buy corporate bonds when credit is tight and attractive yields abound.

There's something about watching and waiting on the bond market to "roll over" that I really enjoy. This is a "when" investment, not an "if" investment. All we have to do is be patient. We know that the feckless, reckless, and stupid management teams running most American companies will borrow too much money and end up in a jam.

It happens every eight years or so. That's about perfect timing for patient investors, as most corporate debt is issued for periods of less than 10 years. You can "lock in" a solid rate of return buying bonds when they go on sale, are trading for less than $0.70 on the dollar, and pay more than 10% annually.

If you begin to do this, I promise, you'll buy far fewer stocks. You'll make a lot more money as an investor. You'll take dramatically fewer risks. And you'll produce way more income.

Now, I know you may be scratching your head at what I've written here. After all, no one has issued more adamant warnings about the bubble that has developed in the bond market. And yes... now is not the time to make big investments in the corporate-bond market.

But the credit cycle is starting to roll over. In 2017, corporate debt is at 45% of GDP – where it has historically peaked. Corporate downgrades and defaults are well above average. And banks have tightened lending standards.

This essay isn't about what to buy today or tomorrow. I want you to recognize the incredible opportunity corporate bonds represent when the conditions are right, when you can get them at the right time and price. Remember, at some point, all markets turn around. And we're getting closer by the day.

After the bond market collapses, most investors want nothing to do with fixed-income investments. That's when we find lots of great opportunities in this market... ones that meet all three of my guidelines for buying corporate bonds.

How do you buy bonds? And which exact ones should you buy? Don't worry. During the last cycle, we made 81%, on average, in 2009-2010. The Rite-Aid bond we recommended way back then is No. 2 in the Stansberry Research Hall of Fame at the bottom of every *Stansberry Digest*.

In November 2015, we launched *Stansberry's Credit Opportunities* to take advantage of the looming crisis. We only recommend buying debt at a discount to par. In two years, we've established positions in 21 bonds. As of late November 2017, we've closed out 11 of those positions for an average gain of 21% and held them for an average of seven months. That's an annualized gain of 36%. There are 10 open positions remaining in our model portfolio for an average gain of 8% (or 11% annualized).

The overall gain for our two-year track record of all 21 actionable recommendations is 15%. That works out to an annualized gain of 24%... with more to come. The average yield on the portfolio was around 7.1%.

If you want to go forth on your own... remember to focus on companies with a lot of high-quality and easily marketable assets.

Judging collateral is a lot different than judging an operating business. You have to think like a pawn dealer: How hard would it be to unload these assets if the idiots running this business really screw the pooch? That's a far different question than figuring out a reasonable price to pay for future cash flows, or brand value, etc.

More and more, I believe bonds are far better investment instruments than stocks for most investors. The funny thing is, most brokerage firms make it difficult for individuals to buy high-yield corporate bonds.

Most won't even tell you what bonds are available. And most will only sell you the bonds you want if you're able to tell them the precise CUSIP number of the bond (its trading symbol).

That's the best indicator of all. Wall Street's smart money doesn't want you figuring out the best deals in the bond market, which, by the way, is vastly larger than the stock market. Interesting, isn't it?

Part VI

How to Earn Crisis-Proof, Inflation-Proof Income Streams in the Stock Market

– Chapter 1 –

The No. 1 Way to Invest for Retirement

What I am about to tell you is without a doubt the No. 1 way to invest for retirement.

Of all the investment ideas we've covered over the years, this stands head and shoulders above the rest. It's the strategy we urge our parents to use. It's the strategy we teach our children.

This strategy produces huge returns. It can turn thousands of dollars into millions of dollars. It's also very low risk. It will allow your investment portfolio to withstand any crisis (just like it did during the financial crisis of 2008).

Rather than worry about money and security in your retirement years, you can use this strategy to live an income-rich retirement.

The neat thing about this strategy is that anyone can use it. It's very simple. Many regular people have used this strategy to make huge fortunes in stocks. You can use it, too.

If you know nothing about the stock market except what is explained in this guide, you'll be a vastly better investor than almost everyone on Wall Street... or any MBA... or anyone on CNBC.

What I'm going to share with you is a "secret" in the sense that few people use it. It's really an "open secret." Nobody has it under lock and key. It's hiding under an invisible blanket of common sense.

When you start putting this secret to work for you, you'll "graduate" into a higher class of investors.

Before you read further, I'd like you to picture a tree...

Once you plant a tree, you don't have to do anything more with it. The tree sinks its roots into the ground and starts growing. All the tree needs is rain, air, and the nutrients in the soil.

You don't have to check on it every day. You leave it alone. You let the awesome forces of nature make the tree stronger and stronger as the years go by. The tree will provide fruit, beauty, and shade for you, your children, and your children's children.

Have that picture in your mind?

That's what using this investment strategy is like.

It's harnessing an unstoppable force of nature to safely build wealth, year after year.

With that picture in mind, let's get started...

– Chapter 2 –

What's Truly Important for Growing Wealth in the Stock Market

If you're reading this, you've probably invested some money in the stock market. You probably have a 401(k), an IRA, or an individual brokerage account.

Once you invest some money, you'll probably start watching a little financial television. You'll probably read financial websites or a few investment magazines.

While reading and listening to financial media, you're sure to encounter dozens of "gurus" who promote lots of different market strategies... and make lots of big predictions. You're sure to see lots of news stories about the economy and the government.

It's a lot to take in. It can all be very confusing.

And for 99 out of 100 people, it is a distraction from what really leads to long-term success in stocks.

You see, the news you read in the paper or hear on CNBC is completely meaningless compared with the idea I'll share with you here.

Most people watch the financial news and think they're doing something important. They're actually just wasting time and getting distracted from what's truly important for making big, safe returns in the stock market.

And what's truly important for growing wealth in stocks is the accumulation of elite, dividend-paying businesses purchased at reasonable prices.

That's it.

It's the most important idea.

It's the "king" of all investment ideas.

It's a thousand times more important than knowing what the economy is doing... or what the government is doing... or what's happening in the news.

Again... what's truly important for growing wealth in stocks is the accumulation of elite, dividend-paying businesses purchased at reasonable prices.

What is an elite business? How can you find it?

And how can one safely and surely generate wealth for you?

You'll find the answers in the pages that follow...

– Chapter 3 –

The Traits of Elite Businesses

There's no set definition of an "elite business." But most smart people agree that elite businesses share some unique traits.

An elite business has a durable competitive advantage over its competitors.

For example, major discount retailer Wal-Mart has a durable competitive advantage because its huge global distribution network allows it to sell goods at unbeatably low prices. It's very, very difficult for smaller firms to compete against it.

An elite business usually has an outstanding brand name.

Coca-Cola is a good example. People associate Coke's logo and name with quality soda all over the world.

An elite business is often the largest business in its industry. When you run your business better than the competition, you usually can't help but become the biggest. McDonald's became America's biggest fast-food chain because it ran a better business than its competitors.

An elite business often sells "basic" products, like food, oil, soda, cigarettes, beer, mouthwash, razor blades, and deodorant. These are things that don't go out of style.

And here's something you don't often hear: **Most of the truly elite businesses sell habit-forming, or even addictive, products**.

If you look at the list of the 20 best-performing U.S. stocks from 1957 through 2003, you'll note many of them sold habit-forming products. It jumps right out at you.

For example, Philip Morris is at the top of the list. It was the top-performing S&P 500 stock from 1957 to 2003. It sold cigarettes, which contain addictive nicotine.

Fortune Brands, which was called American Brands for a while, is on the list. It sold cigarettes and alcohol.

Coca-Cola and PepsiCo are on the list. They sold soda... which is a sugar- and caffeine-delivery vehicle.

Hershey Foods and Tootsie Roll are on the list. They sold chocolate and sugar. Wrigley is on the list. It sold sugary gum, like Big Red and Juicy Fruit.

People love a little sugar rush. It's habit-forming... even addictive.

Many drug companies are on the list. These names include Abbott Labs, Bristol-Myers Squibb, Merck, Wyeth, Schering-Plough, and Pfizer.

People get accustomed to taking certain drugs. Much of the time, those drugs are useful. Sometimes, they are not. I'm not saying they are good or bad. I'm simply pointing out that people get accustomed, even addicted, to taking them.

You can make the case that certain fast foods are addictive as well. Fast-food companies load their food with fat, sugar, and chemicals that make people want more. This is part of the reason McDonald's has been such a corporate success.

The businesses I just mentioned produced more than 13% annual gains for more than three decades.

Those returns are extraordinarily rare in the stock market. You won't find anything better.

An investment of $25,000 in a tax-deferred account that grows 13% per year for 30 years grows to nearly $1 million ($977,897).

Most companies can't sustain 13% annual returns for more than five years. **The businesses I just mentioned sustained those returns for decades**.

And the reason why they did so well is simple...

When people form a habit around a product, it goes a long way toward ensuring repeat business. People get used to certain brands, and they grow resistant to switching.

Also, when people get used to a product and the brand surrounding it, they are more likely to continue buying the product, even if the price increases a little. Both of these help companies sustain long-term sales growth and healthy profit margins. That's good for shareholders.

It's also important to know that when these companies hit upon the right recipes or the right mix of whatever it takes to make good products, they don't have to make large, ongoing investments in the business. They don't have to spend tons of money on more research and development.

Once Coca-Cola hit upon the recipe for Coke, it didn't have to change it. The same goes for Budweiser and Hershey and Tootsie Roll.

When you make a product that people love and develop habits around, you don't tinker with it. You don't have to spend a lot of money on new research and development. You don't have to buy expensive, high-tech equipment.

You can instead spend that money on things that will provide a high return on investment, like marketing, distribution, or manufacturing.

This means a larger percentage of revenues can be sent to shareholders.

Owning the world's top sellers of basic (often habit-forming) products is also ideal for investing in high-growth emerging markets like China and India.

Combined, China and India have about 10 times the population of the United States. Many of those people are at the level of economic development of America during the 1940s... and they are getting a little richer every year. It's one of the biggest investment opportunities in history.

To invest in this trend, I don't want to try to guess what websites will get the most clicks... or what retailer will become popular. That's a very difficult game to play. Those business landscapes will change rapidly.

On the other hand, I'm confident those folks in China and India who are getting a little richer every year will want to enjoy the same habit-forming products Americans have enjoyed for decades.

They'll want to consume more branded soda, cigarettes, beer, liquor, and processed foods.

Owning elite global businesses that serve those growing markets makes a lot of sense.

(By the way... these global sellers of branded, habit-forming consumer goods are the kinds of businesses Warren Buffett always looks to buy. He's a longtime owner of Coca-Cola and candy maker See's Candies.)

– Chapter 4 –

The Secret of High Stock Market Returns

When a great business develops a durable advantage over its competitors, it often begins paying steady and rising dividends.

Dividends are cash payments distributed to a company's shareholders. They are often quoted in dollars per share, as in "Coca-Cola pays a dividend of $1 per share."

Dividends are also quoted in terms of a percent of the current stock price. This percentage is referred to as the "yield." You might say, "Coca-Cola pays a dividend yield of 3%."

In 2012, respected investment research firm Ned Davis Research produced a study that shows why investors should care **a lot** about dividends.

This study contained some of the most valuable data you'll ever see. Understanding this data can make you rich. Not understanding it can cost you years of wasted effort and lots of money.

You shouldn't invest one dime in the stock market unless you understand it.

In the study, Ned Davis Research analyzed the returns of various types of stocks within the benchmark S&P 500 Index from 1972 to 2010.

In this study, Ned Davis Research placed each S&P 500 stock into one of four general categories.

Category one: Companies that were paying dividends and increasing them.

Category two: Companies that were paying dividends, but not increasing them.

Category three: Companies that were reducing or eliminating dividend payments.

Category four: Companies that didn't pay a dividend.

In other words, Ned Davis Research categorized stocks based on their policies of paying cash to shareholders.

You could say two of the categories (reducing dividends or not paying dividends) consisted of businesses that were generally **not good at paying cash to shareholders**.

You could say one category consisted of companies that were **OK at paying cash to shareholders** (paying dividends, but not increasing them).

You could say the fourth category consisted of stocks that were **great at paying ever-increasing amounts of cash to shareholders** (paying dividends and increasing them).

According to the study, companies that paid growing dividends returned an average of 9.6% per year. Companies that were paying dividends but not increasing them returned an average of 7.4% per year.

Companies that did not pay dividends returned an average of 1.7% per year. Companies that were cutting or eliminating their dividends returned -0.5% per year.

Here is that data shown in a table:

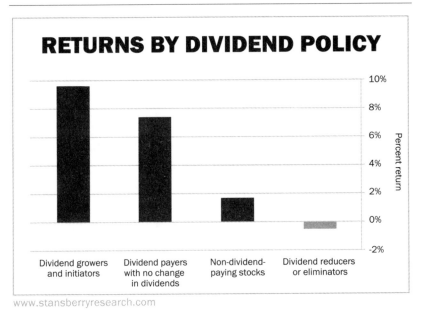

www.stansberryresearch.com

The results of the nearly 40-year study are clear: Companies that are great at paying cash to shareholders perform better than companies that stink at it. As the ability to pay dividends increases, returns go up. As the ability to pay dividends declines, returns go down.

Continuously rising dividends is a mark of business excellence. **And business excellence translates to big shareholder returns**.

"Wait a minute," you might say. "If I only buy stocks that pay dividends, won't I miss out on big growth-stock winners that invest their profits into growing the business instead of paying it to shareholders?"

Yes, you will.

By sticking with dividend-paying stocks, you will miss out on investing in the next Starbucks... or the next Facebook.

But remember, for every winner like Starbucks, there are 1,000 failed coffee chains.

For every winner like Facebook, there are 1,000 failed websites.

It's very, very unlikely that the average investor will be able to consistently find these companies early on... and hold them for years.

Even trained professionals struggle (and often fail) to pick those kinds of winners.

It's *much, much more likely* the average investor will be able to consistently identify companies that sell boring, basic products like soap, burgers, and beer... and pay ever-increasing dividends.

By now, you know those companies are usually found in your refrigerator, cupboard, or medicine cabinet.

If you're interested in building long-term wealth in the stock market, consider changing the way you look at different stocks.

Consider placing each business you come across into one of four simple categories. And only buy businesses that fit into one of those categories: The rising dividend category.

Does the business pay rising dividends, stagnant dividends, no dividends, or is it reducing dividends?

If the business doesn't pay continuously rising dividends, pass on it. Buy the best and ignore the rest!

– Chapter 5 –

The Shortcut for Finding the World's Best Businesses

Now... you can spend a lot of time searching for "elite businesses."

You can study for days and learn how to analyze stocks. You can spend hours going over financial statements.

But if you're like a lot of people, you don't have the interest or the time. You've got a job and a family, and they keep you busy.

The good news is, there's a shortcut around doing all that work.

You can simply look for businesses that have increased their dividends for at least 10 years in a row.

Remember, dividends are cash payments distributed to a company's shareholders. Only businesses with durable competitive advantages can pay increasing dividends for more than a decade.

Out of the more than 5,000 publicly traded businesses, less than 5% meet this high standard of quality.

These businesses are the beachfront real estate of the stock market.

Some legendarily profitable and stable members of the "dividend raiser" club include Coca-Cola, McDonald's, and Wal-Mart... as well as health care company Johnson & Johnson, payroll services company Automatic Data Processing, global courier FedEx, soft-drink maker PepsiCo, manufacturing conglomerate 3M, consumer-products maker Procter & Gamble, and gas giants Chevron and ExxonMobil.

The longer the string of consecutive dividend increases, the more impressive it is. Only truly fantastic businesses with durable competitive advantages can increase their dividends for 20, 30, or even 40 consecutive years.

As of 2017, Wal-Mart has increased its dividend payment every year for 44 years. ExxonMobil has increased its dividend payment every year for more than 35 years. Coca-Cola has increased its dividend payment every year for 55 years.

These businesses paid and increased their dividends through recessions, government shutdowns, wars, and real estate busts. They paid their dividends during the dot-com bust. They paid their dividends during the 2008-2009 financial crisis – the ultimate dividend "stress test."

In terms of consistency, these firms rank just behind the rising sun.

Companies with more than 10 or 20 years of consecutive dividend increases are the strongest, safest companies in the world. As I mentioned, many of these firms sell "basic" products like medicine, soda, food, candy, cigarettes, toothpaste, and deodorant.

Ordinary companies can't raise their dividends for 10 or 20 consecutive years. In fact, they probably won't even exist that long. This is because their business models are shaky, unpredictable, and vulnerable to competition.

The average investor will spend lots of time chasing hot tips from brokers, coworkers, and relatives. He'll chase "get rich quick" schemes. He'll try to pick stocks based on chart patterns. He'll stay up at night worrying about the risky stocks he owns.

It's bizarre behavior when you realize there is a group of elite, dividend-paying businesses available to him. He's choosing Spam over filet mignon.

Instead of owning risky stocks, I like the predictability of owning robust, reliable businesses like McDonald's and Coca-Cola.

I can't pick the next hit website, the next miracle drug, or the next retail fad. But I know it's very, very likely that folks will keep eating burgers, drinking soda, and brushing their teeth.

Again, you can spend lots of time learning how to analyze businesses... You can spend a lot of time searching for them.

Or you can simply "weed out" more than 99% of stocks by focusing on companies with long strings of consecutive dividend increases.

Several lists of these companies are compiled each year. One is called "Dividend Achievers." It's the list of companies that have increased their dividends for at least 10 consecutive years. As of 2017, there were 264 members of this list.

Another list is called "Dividend Aristocrats." It's the list of companies that have increased their dividends for 25 consecutive years. As of 2017, there were only 51 members of this list.

You can think of these lists as "cheat sheets" for finding the world's best businesses.

You work hard for your money. Don't abuse it by investing in low-quality businesses.

Instead of buying unproven businesses based on whims, chart patterns, and hot tips, demand quality from the businesses you buy.

One of the greatest indicators of business quality is at least 10 years of consecutive dividend increases. This is the blue ribbon worn by the best public businesses.

– Chapter 6 –

A Strategy for Buying Elite Businesses at Bargain Prices

Although the businesses I've described are the best on Earth, they suffer share-price selloffs from time to time.

Sometimes, these selloffs are caused by short-term, solvable problems within the individual companies.

Sometimes, these selloffs are caused because the overall stock market goes down in value.

These selloffs are almost always opportunities to buy these firms at bargain prices and start collecting steady dividend payments.

When you buy a car, you want to pay a good price. When you buy a house, you want to pay a good price. You don't want to overpay. You don't want to embarrass yourself by getting ripped off. You want to get value for your dollar.

Yet... when people invest, the idea of paying a good price is often cast aside.

They get excited about a story they read in a magazine... or how much their brother-in-law is making in a stock, and they just buy it.

They don't pay any attention to the prices they're paying... or the value they're getting for their investment dollars.

Warren Buffett often repeats a valuable quote from investment legend Ben Graham: *"Price is what you pay, value is what you get."* That's a great way to put it.

Like many investment concepts, it's helpful to think of it in terms of real estate...

Let's say there's a great house in your neighborhood. It's an attractive house with solid, modern construction and new appliances. It could bring in $30,000 per year in rent. This is the "gross" rental income... or the income you have before subtracting expenses.

If you could buy this house for just $120,000, it would be a good deal.

You could get back your purchase price in gross rental income in just four years ($120,000 / $30,000 = 4).

In this example, we'd say you're paying "four times gross rental income."

Now... let's say you pay $600,000 for that house.

You would get back your purchase price in gross rental income in 20 years ($600,000 / $30,000 = 20).

In this example, we'd say you're paying "20 times gross rental income."

Paying $600,000 is obviously not as good a deal as paying just **$120,000**.

Remember, in this example, we're talking about buying the same house.

We're talking about the same amount of rental income.

In one case, you're paying a good price. You're getting a good deal. You'll recoup your investment in gross rental income in just four years.

In the other case, you're paying a lot more. You're not getting a good deal. It will take you 20 years just to recoup your investment.

And it's all a factor of the price you pay.

It works the same way when investing in a business...

You want to buy at a good price that allows you to get a good return on your investment. You want to avoid buying at a bloated, expensive price.

This is a vital point.

No matter how great a business is, **it can turn out to be a terrible investment if you pay the wrong price**.

If you're not clear on this point, please read through the home example again.

When it comes to buying elite businesses that raise their dividends every year, you can use the company's dividend yield to help you answer the important question: "*Is this business trading for a good price or a bad price?*"

Here's how it works...

When a stock's price goes down and the annual dividend remains the same, the dividend yield rises.

For example, let's say a stock is $50 per share and pays a $2-per-share annual dividend. This represents a yield of 4% (2 / 50 = 4%).

If the stock declines to $40 per share and the dividend payment remains $2 per share, the stock will yield 5% (2 / 40 = 5%).

When a selloff causes an elite dividend-payer to trade near the high end of its historical dividend-yield range, it's a bargain... and it's a good idea to buy shares.

Remember, these companies pay the world's most reliable dividends. Their annual payouts only go one way – UP.

When an elite dividend-payer's share price suffers a decline of more than 15%, consider it "on sale" and buy it.

For example, in the late 2008/early 2009 stock market decline, shares of elite dividend-payer Procter & Gamble fell from $65 to $45 (a decline of 30%).

Procter & Gamble is one of the world's top consumer-products businesses. Every year, it sells billions and billions of dollars' worth of basic, everyday products like Gillette razors, Pampers diapers, Charmin toilet paper, Crest toothpaste, Bounty paper towels, and Tide laundry detergent. It has raised its dividend every year for more than 50 years.

Investors who stepped in to buy this high-quality business after the market decline could have purchased shares at $50.

In the five years that followed, Procter & Gamble climbed to $80 per share.

Its annual dividend grew to $2.57 per share.

This annual dividend represented a 5.1% yield on a purchase price of $50 per share... and that yield will continue rising for many years.

Owning one of the world's best businesses... earning a 5.1% yield on your shares... and collecting a safe income stream that rises every year...

Buying the best at bargain prices is a beautiful thing.

If you have the interest, time, and know-how, you can track these businesses yourself. You can find all the information you need on many free financial websites. Or you can simply pay an advisor or research firm to do it for you.

Remember, you can make a bad investment in a great business if you pay a stupid price. View your investment purchases just like you would the purchase of a home, a car, or a computer.

Get good value for your investment dollar. And when an elite dividend-payer sells off for some reason, see it as an opportunity to buy quality at a bargain price.

– Chapter 7 –

Why Owners of Elite, Dividend-Paying Businesses Don't Worry About 'the Market'

When you realize that your No. 1 job as an investor is to accumulate as many shares as possible of elite, dividend-paying businesses, you "graduate" into a higher class of investor.

You also experience a lot less stress than the average investor. Let me explain...

Few people belong to this exclusive class because most folks are obsessed with short-term gratification.

They pore over tiny market movements, news releases, CNBC clips, and other things that are meaningless in the "big picture."

These people are always busy trying to get the market to do something for them... instead of using the greatest power in all of investing.

That power is TIME.

And if used properly, time causes extraordinary things to happen to your portfolio.

Time allows you to earn huge yields from elite, dividend-paying businesses. Time makes it so you don't care about the moods of the stock market.

Here's how it works...

Let's say you buy Reliable Breweries (a fictional company), which is an elite, dividend-paying business, for $20 per share. It has increased its dividend payment every year for the past 30 years. It pays a 5% annual dividend, or $1 per share.

Now, let's say that dividend grows at 10% per year for the next 10 years. (This rate of dividend growth is common with elite businesses.)

After 10 years of growing at 10% per year, your annual dividend is now almost 13% of your initial investment. After 15 years of growing at 10%, your annual dividend is 21% of your initial investment. After 20 years of growing at 10%, your annual dividend is 34% of your initial investment.

Now... do you think a guy earning a safe 13% yield with one of the world's best businesses cares about a stock market correction?

Do you think he cares about a 5% decline in home prices? Do you think he cares about some economic news story on financial television?

No way.

He's comfortable knowing that no matter what the stock market does, folks are still going to be buying products from Reliable Breweries.

He knows the broad market could decline by 20% and he would still get that 13% yield on his shares. They could shut the market down for a year, and he'd still get his money.

That's the peace of mind accumulators of elite, dividend-paying businesses enjoy.

By combining the power of an elite, dividend-paying business and the power of time, you are able to generate massive yields on your original investment. You just have to let time work its magic.

This concept is very important to understand... so please think about a few more questions...

If you're earning a 13% (and growing) yield on a stock, do you care if the share price falls 10%?

Do you care if oil climbs $10 or $20 per barrel?

Do you care that this guy or that guy is predicting a stock market decline? No way.

No matter what stories the media is hyping, the "biggies" of the corporate world – companies like McDonald's and Coca-Cola – will still be No. 1 in their industries.

They'll still have giant, insurmountable competitive advantages.

They'll still have thick profit margins. They'll still generate huge cash flows.

They'll still direct a portion of those cash flows to shareholders through ever-increasing dividends.

Their longtime shareholders will still earn 13%-plus yields on their original investments.

For most folks, trying to trade in and out of stocks takes up too much time. It generates high fees. It produces losses. It causes sleepless nights. It drains mental energy.

But if you own a collection of elite, dividend-paying businesses, you won't worry about much.

You sleep well knowing that all you need is TIME. Time allows dividend growth to work its magic.

Think of it like planting a money tree... and remember what I said at the start of this section...

> Once you plant a tree, you don't have to do anything more with it. The tree sinks its roots into the ground and starts to grow. All the tree needs are rain, air, and the nutrients in the soil.
>
> You don't have to check on it every day. You leave it alone. You let the awesome forces of nature make the tree stronger and stronger as the years go by. The tree will provide fruit, beauty, and shade for you, your children, and your children's children.

Buy an elite, dividend-paying business at a good price, leave it alone, and it will grow large in your portfolio.

Given enough time, it will throw off 5%... 10%... even 25% annual dividends on your original purchase price.

It will grow into a large money tree you and your family can enjoy for decades.

As you go through your investment career, keep in mind your No. 1 job: **To accumulate as many shares as possible in great businesses purchased at reasonable prices**.

– Chapter 8 –

Elite Businesses Allow You to Harness the Power of Compounding

Getting paid a reliable and growing dividend is a great thing.

As I mentioned, over time, it can produce 13%-plus yields on your initial investment.

But there's a way to make this great idea even better...

Elite, dividend-paying companies like McDonald's and Coca-Cola allow you to harness the most powerful investment force on the planet.

This force is called "compounding."

Compounding occurs when you place a chunk of money into an invesment that pays you a return on your money. But instead of taking the returns and spending them, you "reinvest" them... and buy more of the investment.

By doing this, your dividends earn more dividends and your interest earns more interest.

You can think of compounding returns through dividend reinvestment like rolling a snowball down a hill. As the snowball gets larger, it's able to gather more snow... which enables it to get larger... which enables it to gather more snow... which enables it to get larger... and so on.

Eventually, you build a snowball the size of a house.

Compounding is the ultimate way for the "little guy" to safely build wealth in the stock market.

245

Given enough time, a good compounding vehicle (like a Dividend Aristocrat) will turn tens of thousands of dollars into millions of dollars.

For example, let's say you invest $10,000 in an investment that pays a 5% dividend. Your intention is to compound over the long term.

In Year 1, a $10,000 investment paying 5% in dividends will pay you $500. You take this money and buy $500 more of the investment.

In Year 2, your investment has grown to $10,500 but still earns 5%. That year, you'll earn $525 in dividends... which you can use to buy more of the investment.

In Year 3, your investment has grown to $11,025, but still earns 5%. At the end of that year, you'll earn $551.25 in dividends... which you can use to buy more of the investment.

You can see how it works.

After 20 years of compounding, a stake of $10,000 throwing off 5% in dividends will grow to $26,533.

After 30 years, it will grow to $43,219. After 40 years, it will grow to $70,400.

And remember, this number assumes no further money is added to the program as the years go by... or that the investment produces any capital gains.

As you can see, long-term compounding produces extraordinary effects.

It's a very important concept for young people to learn... because they have the power of TIME on their side.

The longer you can compound, the more extraordinary the results.

The following example shows just how extraordinary the results can be...

Consider two investors, Robert and Sally.

Robert opens a tax-deferred retirement account at age 26. He invests $3,000 per year in this account for 40 consecutive years. Robert stops contributing at age 65. His account grows at 9% per year.

Sally opens a tax-deferred retirement account at age 18. She invests $3,000 per year in this account for eight consecutive years. After those eight years, she makes no more contributions to her retirement account. Her account grows at 9% per year.

The results of these two approaches are below... and they are extraordinary:

Age	Robert Contribution	Year-End Value	Sally Contribution	Year-End Value
16	$0	$0	$0	$0
17	$0	$0	$0	$0
18	$0	$0	$3,000	$3,270
19	$0	$0	$3,000	$6,834
20	$0	$0	$3,000	$10,719
21	$0	$0	$3,000	$14,954
22	$0	$0	$3,000	$19,570
23	$0	$0	$3,000	$24,601
24	$0	$0	$3,000	$30,085
25	$0	$0	$3,000	$36,063
26	$3,000	$3,270	$0	$39,309
27	$3,000	$6,834	$0	$42,847
28	$3,000	$10,719	$0	$46,703
29	$3,000	$14,954	$0	$50,906
30	$3,000	$19,570	$0	$55,488
31	$3,000	$24,601	$0	$60,481
32	$3,000	$30,085	$0	$65,925
33	$3,000	$36,063	$0	$71,858
34	$3,000	$42,579	$0	$78,325
35	$3,000	$49,681	$0	$85,374
36	$3,000	$57,422	$0	$93,058
37	$3,000	$65,860	$0	$101,433
38	$3,000	$75,058	$0	$110,562

39	$3,000	$85,083	$0	$120,513
40	$3,000	$96,010	$0	$131,359
41	$3,000	$107,921	$0	$143,182
42	$3,000	$120,904	$0	$156,068
43	$3,000	$135,055	$0	$170,114
44	$3,000	$150,480	$0	$185,424
45	$3,000	$167,294	$0	$202,112
46	$3,000	$185,620	$0	$220,303
47	$3,000	$205,596	$0	$240,130
48	$3,000	$227,369	$0	$261,742
49	$3,000	$251,103	$0	$285,298
50	$3,000	$276,972	$0	$310,975
51	$3,000	$305,169	$0	$338,963
52	$3,000	$335,905	$0	$369,470
53	$3,000	$369,406	$0	$402,722
54	$3,000	$405,923	$0	$438,967
55	$3,000	$445,726	$0	$478,474
56	$3,000	$489,111	$0	$521,536
57	$3,000	$536,401	$0	$568,475
58	$3,000	$587,947	$0	$619,637
59	$3,000	$644,132	$0	$675,405
60	$3,000	$705,374	$0	$736,191
61	$3,000	$772,128	$0	$802,448
62	$3,000	$844,889	$0	$874,669
63	$3,000	$924,199	$0	$953,389
64	$3,000	$1,010,647	$0	$1,039,194
65	$3,000	$1,104,876	$0	$1,132,721
Less Total Invested	**-$120,000**			**-$24,000**
Net Earnings	**$984,876**			**$1,108,721**
Return on Money	**8-fold**			**46-fold**

Sally made just eight contributions of $3,000, for a total of $24,000 invested. Robert made 40 contributions of $3,000, for a total of $120,000 invested.

However, Sally started at 18 years of age and Robert started at 26 years of age. Sally started eight years earlier. And those eight extra years of compounding are worth more than all of Robert's 32 years of extra contributions.

Despite a much smaller total contribution, Sally ended up with more money... and a much, much bigger return on her investment.

This example shows why compounding is such a powerful idea to teach children. They have the ultimate advantage of TIME.

This piece of knowledge is one of the greatest financial gifts you could ever give your children.

In order to put your compounding plans on "autopilot," consider using something called a **"dividend reinvestment plan," also called a DRIP.**

A DRIP is just what it sounds like. It's a plan that takes the dividends you earn and reinvests them into buying more stock.

Once you set up a DRIP, you don't have to do a thing. Again, think of a DRIP as a way to put your compounding plan on "autopilot."

You can ask any stock broker to institute a DRIP for you. Any reputable online broker will do it for you. It's a simple process. You can find directions on your broker's website or call the customer service department.

– Chapter 9 –

Elite Dividend-Payers: The Cure for the Biggest Mistake Income Investors Make

Amateur investors often bring up a common objection to buying elite, dividend-paying businesses.

Acting on this objection often leads them into very risky investments.

Most elite, dividend-payers sport annual dividend yields in the neighborhood of 2%-5%. And remember, these yields are incredibly safe and reliable. They rise every year.

In addition to elite dividend-payers, the stock market contains groups of businesses that pay annual yields of 6%... 8%... 10%... even 12%.

The amateur looks at these numbers and says, "Why buy a business that yields 4% when I can buy one that yields 8%?" And then the amateur makes one of the biggest investment mistakes in the world.

He "chases" yield.

There's a classic piece of investment wisdom about "chasing yield." It goes: "*More money has been lost chasing yield than at the barrel of a gun.*"

"Chasing yield" is the act of buying specific stocks simply because they offer high yields... while ignoring vital business factors.

Some businesses engage in risky business ventures or take on lots of debt in order to pay high yields. Finance and real estate companies often do this.

Some businesses own oil and gas wells and pay dividends from the production. Those dividend payouts are often totally dependent on oil and gas prices staying elevated.

They can be incredibly volatile.

These businesses are usually very dangerous for the average investor.

For example, there is a group of companies whose chief business activity is borrowing money at low interest rates... and then using that borrowed money to buy mortgages that pay higher interest rates. They make money from the "spread."

One of the largest and most popular of these companies is Annaly Capital Management.

Annaly is probably operated by good people. But because it borrows lots of money to buy mortgages, its business and its dividend yield are very volatile. Small changes in the business (like how much it has to pay to borrow money) can cause enormous changes in shareholder returns.

Here is a chart of Annaly's dividend payments from late 2007 to late 2017. As you can see, these payments were incredibly volatile between 2008 and 2014.

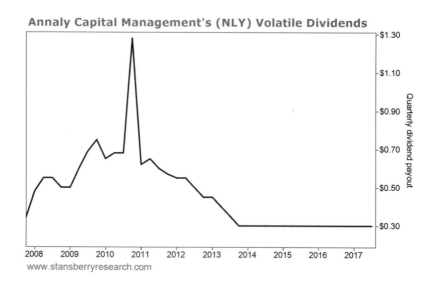

Annaly Capital Management's (NLY) Volatile Dividends

The volatile nature of Annaly's dividend payments leads to volatile share-price movement. Next is a chart of Annaly's share price during the same time period (late 2007 to late 2017). Note the drop from more than $20 per share to $10 per share.

Annaly Capital Management (NLY)

www.stansberryresearch.com

Or... consider the performance of the San Juan Basin Royalty Trust from 2011 to 2013. At the time, this trust was one of the biggest and most popular trusts that owned natural gas assets.

From mid-2011 to mid-2012, the price of natural gas dropped around 50%. Because the San Juan Basin Royalty Trust derived its revenue from natural gas, its shares dropped as well. As you can see from the next chart, they fell from nearly $28 to around $12 per share... and later dropped below $5.

San Juan Basin Royalty Trust (SJT)

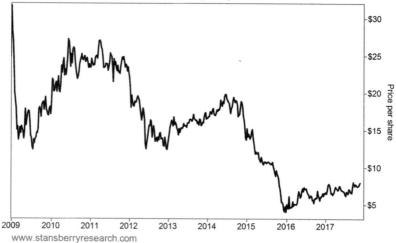

www.stansberryresearch.com

Also consider the performance of Enerplus. In 2011, it was one of the biggest and most popular owners of oil and gas wells... and paid dividends out of production.

In 2011, crude oil fell from $110 per barrel to $85 per barrel. This decline helped crush Enerplus shares. As you can see, they fell from $32 per share to less than $12 per share. Shares sold off further with the 2015 decline in oil.

Enerplus (ERF)

www.stansberryresearch.com

The examples of Annaly, San Juan Basin, and Enerplus are not unique. And I'm not picking on these particular businesses.

This story plays out over and over in the stock market... with dozens and dozens of companies.

Unsuspecting investors see a company offering a very high yield and they buy it. They don't do any research to determine if the business model is risky or not. In almost every case, it is.

Some investors are good at timing their purchases of these volatile businesses. They buy them when they are deeply out of favor with most investors.

However, the average investor almost always buys these businesses at the wrong time: near peaks in share prices. He picks up 8% in dividends and then loses 30% on the share-price drop.

The individual investor is much, much better off owning stable businesses that pay out reliable and growing dividends. You don't trade in and out of elite dividend-payers. There's no frequent buying and selling. There's no worry that the share price will fall 30%. There's no dangerous leverage. You simply buy them and begin building wealth the low-stress way.

While the dividends and share price of Annaly were bouncing up and down, elite dividend-payers like Coca-Cola and McDonald's were paying steady and rising dividends.

– Chapter 10 –

Why Elite, Dividend-Paying Businesses Are the Ultimate 'Wealth Defense'

If you're like a lot of folks, you're worried about inflation... and the danger it presents for people saving for retirement or already in retirement.

You might also be worried another financial crisis – like the upcoming Debt Jubilee – is wrecking your investments.

If you're one of these people (and there's a good chance you are), the "no brainer" decision for you is to own the elite, dividend-paying businesses.

Owning an elite, dividend-paying business is a good inflation defense because the business' strong brand and loyal customer base will allow it to raise prices along with inflation. Its dividend will often increase at a faster rate than inflation, so the value of your income stream remains intact.

These companies are safer, better places to park long-term wealth than any currency or any government bond. They are better for parking long-term wealth than precious metals.

There are several major reasons why they're incredible vehicles for your money...

For one, **buying a great business is extremely cheap and easy**. You don't get hit with big fees and commissions when you buy and sell them. You can't say that about real estate or art. Buying a great business through an online broker will cost you less than lunch at most restaurants.

Two, **holding a great business is extremely cheap and easy**. It's as easy as holding cash in the bank. There are no storage costs. There are no transportation costs. You don't have to get a safe-deposit box or a home safe, like you might do with gold or diamonds.

Three, **shares of a great business are liquid and freely traded**. There's a huge market for these business. It's open most every business day.

Four, elite, **dividend-paying businesses also pay out reliable, extremely safe income to their shareholders**.

And finally, **great businesses are great inflation-defense vehicles**. They have long histories of rising in value when paper currencies decline in value.

This is one of the most important aspects of these stocks...

You see, governments have a long history of debasing currencies.

When governments want to pay for big social programs or wars, they often print up extra currency units (like dollars). Every currency unit that is printed devalues the existing currency units. This is called "inflating" the money supply.

Inflation is a way for governments to quietly clip small bits of value from your bank account and your wallet.

Inflation is one of the greatest dangers a person saving for retirement faces. It can crush the future buying power of the money you save today.

This is why owning great businesses is so important. Great businesses hold their value through inflationary periods.

Warren Buffett figured this out a long time ago.

Buffett urges people who are worried about paper-currency declines to own world-class businesses. He knows that owning great businesses is a better inflation-defense than owning gold.

I agree with Buffett on this point. The numbers prove it. Owning great businesses is better than gold when it comes to preserving and growing wealth over the long term.

Consider that from the start of 1990 through October 2016 – a time period that includes booms and busts for both stocks and gold – gold returned roughly 205%.

Now consider during that time...

- ExxonMobil returned 1,377%.

- Wal-Mart returned 1,662%.

- Coca-Cola returned 1,438%.

- Johnson & Johnson returned 2,742%.

- McDonald's returned 2,021%.

(Note: These numbers factor in dividend reinvestment.)

Keep in mind... these companies were well-established enterprises in 1990. It wasn't like you were buying speculative startups.

The numbers are clear. Owning elite businesses that generate consistent dividends is a better long-term strategy than owning gold.

If you're concerned about inflation or another financial crisis, I encourage you to think about this idea... and how the world's greatest investor, Warren Buffett, approaches it.

Sure... own some gold. Own some real estate. But keep in mind the proven wealth-building power of owning the world's best businesses.

– Chapter 11 –

A Beautiful View of Your Investment Backyard

As great as the idea of "planting money trees" is, you're unlikely to use this strategy at the start of your investment career.

The reason is that this investment approach is boring. You're simply buying the world's best businesses and holding them for years and years.

Checking in on these businesses usually amounts to hearing about modest increases in profit... and increases in dividend payments.

These companies typically don't report big "breakthroughs" that could double profits in a year. They just report steady sales growth and relentless dividend increases. They do this year after year after year.

This approach doesn't provide much "action." And when it comes to investing, most people seek action. They pursue lots of hot tips. They look to strike it rich with one big win. They simply can't bring themselves to pursue such a boring strategy.

You also might get overwhelmed by all the information out there on how to invest. There are dozens of investment gurus touting their strategies. There are hundreds of investment books. There are thousands of investment websites.

If you achieve great results with other strategies, congratulations. But if you're one of the many investors who has found lots of "action" – but little success – with exciting strategies, I hope you'll come around to the idea of owning elite, dividend-paying businesses.

Once you come around and commit to a lifetime of accumulating these businesses at reasonable prices, you'll eventually have a beautiful view of your "investment backyard"...

At the end of your investment career, you'll have a large collection of elite, dividend-paying businesses... throwing off regular cash dividends. *You'll have an orchard of money trees in your backyard.*

The branches of your money trees will be heavy with fruit every year. One "tree" will yield 20% on your original investment... one will yield 25% on your original investment... one will yield 30% on your original investment... and so on.

Broad market corrections won't concern you. The latest government drama won't concern you.

You'll sleep well at night knowing your elite businesses will continue to pay out regular cash dividends.

You'll have a large and growing portfolio of the world's best soda companies, the world's best energy companies, the world's best food companies, etc.

Instead of a fancy art collection or a car collection, you'll have a money tree collection.

For emphasis, let's go over it one last time...

*If you commit to a lifetime of accumulating elite, dividend-pay-*ing businesses purchased at reasonable prices, you're virtually guaranteed to build significant wealth in the stock market. *And you will build that wealth safely.*

This is the world's No. 1 way to invest for retirement.

It's the closest thing there is to having money trees growing in your backyard.

Final Thoughts

The Time to Protect Yourself and Your Family Is NOW

There's no denying the major problems in America today or the likely solution.

The majority of Americans are facing record amounts of consumer debt. Their wages have remained stagnant (or fallen) compared with inflation. And the only ways out are to pay their debts, to default, or to have them forgiven with a Debt Jubilee.

Today, America's low-income households don't have the funds to service the money they owe. It's mathematically impossible. And politicians will never allow tens of millions of our poorest citizens to go bankrupt.

So the only solution left is a Debt Jubilee.

The last two times this happened – in the 1930s and 1970s – the U.S. dollar fell in value, inflation soared, and the stock market plummeted.

This time, millions of investors, pensioners, insurance customers, and creditors will lose a fortune. Stocks will collapse. Dozens of companies will go bankrupt.

The government might call it a "National Restoration" or "Patriotic Solvency."

They might pass an act like they did in 1841... or invoke an executive order as they did in 1933 (Executive Order No. 6102)... or simply issue a mandate to the secretary of the Treasury as they did in 1971.

But the Jubilee will come. All you can do is prepare yourself for this inevitability.

Stay away from the most dangerous companies in America today, protect your retirement accounts, invest in a safe, hedged portfolio, own trophy assets and elite, dividend-paying businesses... and you will not only survive the Jubilee – you will be among the select few to profit from it.

Good investing,

Porter Stansberry
Founder, Stansberry Research